CLASSICS IN EDUCATION
Lawrence A. Cremin, General Editor

☆　　☆　　☆

THE REPUBLIC AND THE SCHOOL
Horace Mann on the Education of Free Men
Edited by Lawrence A. Cremin

AMERICAN IDEAS ABOUT ADULT EDUCATION
1710–1951
Edited by C. Hartley Grattan

DEWEY ON EDUCATION
Introduction and Notes by Martin S. Dworkin

THE SUPREME COURT AND EDUCATION
Edited by David Fellman

INTERNATIONAL EDUCATION
A Documentary History
Edited by David G. Scanlon

CRUSADE AGAINST IGNORANCE
Thomas Jefferson on Education
Edited by Gordon C. Lee

CHINESE EDUCATION UNDER COMMUNISM
Edited by Chang-Tu Hu

CHARLES W. ELIOT AND POPULAR EDUCATION
Edited by Edward A. Krug

WILLIAM T. HARRIS ON EDUCATION
(in preparation)
Edited by Martin S. Dworkin

THE *EMILE* OF JEAN JACQUES ROUSSEAU
Selections
Translated and Edited by William Boyd

THE MINOR EDUCATIONAL WRITINGS OF
JEAN JACQUES ROUSSEAU
Selected and Translated by William Boyd

PSYCHOLOGY AND THE SCIENCE OF EDUCATION
Selected Writings of Edward L. Thorndike
Edited by Geraldine M. Joncich

THE NEW-ENGLAND PRIMER
Introduction by Paul Leicester Ford

BENJAMIN FRANKLIN ON EDUCATION
Edited by John Hardin Best

THE COLLEGES AND THE PUBLIC
1787–1862
Edited by Theodore Rawson Crane

TRADITIONS OF AFRICAN EDUCATION
Edited by David G. Scanlon

NOAH WEBSTER'S AMERICAN SPELLING BOOK
Introductory Essay by Henry Steele Commager

VITTORINO DA FELTRE
AND OTHER HUMANIST EDUCATORS
By William Harrison Woodward
Foreword by Eugene F. Rice, Jr.

DESIDERIUS ERASMUS CONCERNING
THE AIM AND METHOD OF EDUCATION
By William Harrison Woodward
Foreword by Craig R. Thompson

JOHN LOCKE ON EDUCATION
Edited by Peter Gay

Crusade
Against Ignorance

THOMAS JEFFERSON ON EDUCATION

Edited, with an Introduction and Notes, by
GORDON C. LEE

CLASSICS IN

No. 6

EDUCATION

BUREAU OF PUBLICATIONS
TEACHERS COLLEGE, COLUMBIA UNIVERSITY
NEW YORK

© 1961 by Teachers College
Columbia University

Third printing, 1964

Library of Congress Catalog Card
Number 61–10961

Printed in the United States of America

Contents

LEARNING AND LIBERTY:
THE JEFFERSONIAN TRADITION
IN EDUCATION
by Gordon C. Lee   1

1. THE PRECIOUS BLESSING OF LIBERTY   27
   *The Declaration of Independence as Adopted
      by Congress, July 4, 1776*   28
   To James Madison, December 20, 1787   33
   To Francis Hopkinson, March 13, 1789   38
   To James Madison, November 17, 1798   41
   The Kentucky Resolutions of 1798   42
   First Inaugural Address, March 4, 1801   50
   To Thomas Seymour, February 11, 1807   55
   To Monsieur N. G. Dufief, April 19, 1814   56

2. THE FREE EXERCISE OF RELIGION   59
   Notes on the State of Virginia, *Query XVII*   60
   A Bill for Establishing Religious Freedom   66
   *To Messrs. Nehemiah Dodge, Ephraim Rob-
      bins, and Stephen S. Nelson, A Committee
      of the Danbury Baptist Association, in the
      State of Connecticut, January 1, 1802*   69
   To Rev. Samuel Miller, January 23, 1808   70
   To P. H. Wendover, March 13, 1815   71
   *Annual Report of the Board of Visitors of the
      University of Virginia, October 7, 1822*   75
   To Doctor Thomas Cooper, November 2, 1822   77

3. THE GENERAL DIFFUSION
   OF KNOWLEDGE   81
   *A Bill for the More General Diffusion of
   Knowledge*   83

   Notes on the State of Virginia, *Query XIV*   92
   To George Wythe, August 13, 1786   97
   To Edward Carrington, January 16, 1787   101

4. THE USEFUL SCIENCES IN THEIR
   HIGHEST DEGREE   104
   To John Banister, Jr., October 15, 1785   106
   To John Adams, July 5, 1814   109
   To George Ticknor, November 25, 1817   112
   *Report of the Commissioners Appointed to Fix
   the Site of the University of Virginia, &c*   114
   To Joseph C. Cabell, February 3, 1825   133
   *Minutes of the Board of Visitors of the Univer-
   sity of Virginia, March 4, 1825*   136
   To William B. Giles, December 26, 1825   137

5. HEALTH, LEARNING, VIRTUE   139
   *To Thomas Mann Randolph, Jr.,
   August 27, 1786*   140
   *To Peter Carr, with Enclosure,
   August 10, 1787*   144
   To Martha Jefferson, March 28, 1787   151
   To Nathaniel Burwell, March 14, 1818   153
   *To Thomas Jefferson Randolph,
   November 24, 1808*   155

EPILOGUE   160
   To John Adams, October 28, 1813   160

Preface

No series called "classics in education" could be complete without its volume devoted to Thomas Jefferson. More clearly than anyone else of his time, this eighteenth-century philosopher and statesman perceived the crucial role of education in the life of a free society. "Enlighten the people generally," he wrote to his friend Du Pont de Nemours in 1816, "and tyranny and oppressions of body and mind will vanish like evil spirits at the dawn of day." A century and a half later, we are less naïve, perhaps, about the powers of popular enlightenment, but we share Jefferson's faith none the less. For popular education may not have guaranteed men freedom—Nazi Germany, after all, was one of the most literate nations in history—but there has been no true freedom in the modern world without it. Today, as in Jefferson's time, any nation that expects to be ignorant and free, and in a state of civilization, does indeed expect what never was and never will be.

LAWRENCE A. CREMIN

Learning and Liberty:
The Jeffersonian Tradition
in Education

By GORDON C. LEE

I

In Western history many of the most influential considerations of educational theory, of fundamental educational policy, have been basically political. Similarly, many of the most significant discussions of politics, of ideals and systems of government, have been anchored in—or at least accompanied by—considerations of the education necessary to the realization of such political ideals. Plato, Aristotle, Cicero among the ancients, Locke, Rousseau, and Dewey among the moderns, come to mind. Certainly not the least in any such listing, and perhaps the outstanding instance of this tendency in American letters or philosophy, is Thomas Jefferson.

Few men in any time, and none in the United States, have so consistently or so fruitfully championed the life of the mind and the relation of that life to the good of society. Few have labored more diligently, here or elsewhere, to design and establish the policies and the institutions for learning and teaching called for by that commitment. And surely no one has more consummately set forth the crucial dependence of representative republican government upon full and systematic enlightenment. "Preach, my dear sir, a crusade against ignorance; establish and improve the law for educating the common people." So wrote Thomas Jefferson in 1786 to his beloved mentor in the study of law, George Wythe. Seldom can a man more dramatically, more persistently, and

1

more effectively have practiced what he himself proclaimed for, as the selections reproduced in this volume
attest, Thomas Jefferson's entire life was just such a
crusade.

Of the men closely associated with the founding of
the republic only Benjamin Franklin can be said to have
approached Jefferson in degree of concern for education.
But even here a marked and significant difference must
be noted, for Franklin, democrat though he clearly was,
saw the necessity for education primarily in economic
and immediately practical terms. Jefferson, on the other
hand, utilitarian though he certainly and proudly was,
conceived of education first and foremost as the *sine qua
non* of a truly viable democracy, as the inescapable
prerequisite to any intelligent popular rule. Dumas Malone writes that "His chief concern was for the attain
ment of liberty, and this provides the best single clue,
not only to his motives in the Revolution but also to his
entire career." [1] And liberty without enlightenment
seemed to Jefferson a contradiction in concepts, an

1 Dumas Malone, *Jefferson The Virginian* (Boston: Little, Brown,
1948), p. 179. This is the first volume of a projected five-volume
series, *Jefferson and His Times*, which bids fair to become the
most authoritative and definitive biography of Thomas Jefferson yet
written. The second volume, *Jefferson and the Rights of Man*, has
also appeared (1951) carrying the history through the re-election of
Washington in 1792. A surprisingly small number of biographies of
Jefferson have been published, despite a significant amount of research dealing with various aspects of his multisided career. Jefferson's early years are extensively treated in Marie Kimball, *Jefferson:
The Road to Glory, 1743 to 1776*, and *Jefferson: War and Peace,
1776 to 1784* (New York: Coward-McCann, 1943 and 1947). Jefferson's entire life has been most recently recounted in Nathan Schach-
ner, *Thomas Jefferson*, two volumes (New York: Appleton-Century-
Crofts, 1951), and in the three-volume work of Claude G. Bowers,
The Young Jefferson, 1743–1789, Jefferson and Hamilton, and
Jefferson in Power (Boston: Houghton Mifflin, 1945, 1925, and 1936).
The Bowers work tends to focus somewhat narrowly upon the
political activity which surrounded Jefferson's life while the Schach-
ner account, though less dramatically written, shows more balance
and greater depth. Perhaps the most useful one-volume treatment is
that by Gilbert Chinard, *Thomas Jefferson, The Apostle of Ameri-
canism* (Boston: Little, Brown, 1943, or Ann Arbor Paperbacks,
1957). Others are Saul K. Padover, *Jefferson* (New York: Harcourt,

anomaly. Indeed, as he once wrote, "Science is more important in a republican than in any other government."

Jefferson seems to have been acutely conscious of the revolutionary and experimental nature of the new American scheme. He was himself of the American West of the eighteenth century; he became profoundly aware of the elemental differences in human circumstance between the Old World and the New; and he clearly foreshadowed Lincoln's suggestion of the American experience as perhaps the last best hope of earth. One cannot read at all extensively from the Jefferson papers[2] with-

---

Brace, 1942, or, as abridged, New York: New American Library, 1952), and Phillips Russell, *Jefferson: Champion of the Free Mind* (New York: Dodd, Mead, 1956).

A most useful supplement to the present volume, which contains almost the entire *Autobiography* and various additional personal accounts, is Adrienne Koch and William Peden, *The Life and Selected Writings of Thomas Jefferson* (New York: Random House, Modern Library, 1944). This book also provides an extensive and well-chosen collection of the Jefferson papers and letters.

2 There have been several major publications of the Jefferson papers and writings. The last of these, which will clearly supersede all the others, is *The Papers of Thomas Jefferson*, edited by Julian P. Boyd (Princeton, N. J.: Princeton University Press, 1950 *et seq.*). Fourteen of a projected fifty volumes of this magnificent work have appeared carrying the Jefferson correspondence through March 1789. The present anthology relies on the Boyd edition wherever possible, but for materials not yet available in that series, the following editions have been utilized:

Paul L. Ford, ed., *The Writings of Thomas Jefferson*, 10 volumes (New York: G. P. Putnam's Sons, 1892–1899).

Andrew A. Lipscomb and A. E. Bergh, eds., *The Writings of Thomas Jefferson*, 20 volumes (Washington, D. C.: Thomas Jefferson Memorial Association, 1903).

James D. Richardson, *A Compilation of the Messages and Papers of the Presidents, 1789–1897*, Vol. I (Washington, D. C.: Government Printing Office, 1896).

Henry A. Washington, ed., *The Writings of Thomas Jefferson*, 9 volumes (New York: Riker, Thorne, 1854).

Also useful are the following single-volume editions of the works of Jefferson:

Philip S. Foner, *The Basic Writings of Thomas Jefferson* (New York: Wiley, 1944).

Saul K. Padover. *The Complete Jefferson* (New York: Tudor, 1943).

out a deep sense that one is dealing with a man suffused with a sense of destiny,[3] and, for Jefferson, the realization of that destiny required boldness, imagination, and faith in the ultimate outcome. At the center of that faith stood the school.

The monumental influence of Thomas Jefferson upon the American tradition and upon education is attributable, of course, to the remarkable combination of genius, interest, and opportunity. As every schoolboy should know, Jefferson's career in public life stands quite unequaled in American annals: member for Albemarle County of the Virginia legislature (colonial and state), delegate to the Continental Congress, Governor of Virginia, Minister to France, Secretary of State, Vice President, and two terms as President. All this was followed by nearly two decades as elder statesman, from whom advice, opinions, and support were avidly sought from all quarters, European as well as American. Such a record of experience and responsibility could hardly fail to leave a giant imprint upon a civilization at any stage, and especially so in its infancy.[4]

But the scope and power of Jefferson's influence are

3 In a letter to Joseph Priestley, the eminent English scholar, dated June 19, 1802, Jefferson observed: "It is impossible not to be sensible that we are acting for all mankind; that circumstances imposed on us the duty of proving what is the degree of freedom and self-government in which a society may venture to leave its individual members." (Ford, 8:159).

4 For valuable general treatments of the period which give the setting for the Jefferson writings, see, for example, Henry Adams, *The United States in 1800* (Ithaca, N. Y.: Cornell University Press, 1955), which is a reprint of the opening chapters of Adams' monumental *History of the United States during the First Administration of Thomas Jefferson* (New York: Scribner's, 1889); Alfred H. Kelly and Winfred A. Harbison, *The American Constitution: Its Origins & Development*, 2 volumes (New York: Norton, 1948), especially Chapters 3–9; Evarts B. Greene, *The Revolutionary Generation, 1763–1790* (New York: Macmillan, 1943); Vernon L. Parrington, *Main Currents in American Thought*, Volume I: *The Colonial Mind, 1620–1800* (New York: Harcourt, Brace, 1927, or Harvest Books, 1954); John R. Krout, *The United States to 1865* (New York: Barnes & Noble, 1953); J. Franklin Jameson, *The American Revolution Considered as a Social Movement* (Princeton, N. J.: Princeton University Press, 1926, or Boston: Beacon Press, 1956).

explained only as we also take account of his incredible many-sidedness, his wondrous versatility, his almost boundless interests, and his orchestra of talents. Again, Franklin is the only figure in American history with whom, in these respects, he is justly compared; and it is not surprising that, both at home and abroad, Jefferson was generally regarded as the automatic successor to the great Philadelphian's mantle. It is impossible to do more here than hint at the universality of Jefferson's range: We see him en route to assume the vice-presidency carrying a box full of mastodon bones to present to the American Philosophical Society, of which he had recently been elected president (a post he was to hold uninterruptedly for twenty years); we hear him playing a miniature fiddle which he had especially made for use on his travels, so that he might play without disturbance to others, for "Music is the passion of my soul"; we watch him transfixed before the classic Maison Carée at Nîmes and recommending this "most beautiful and precious morsel of architecture left us by antiquity" as the model for the new capitol for Virginia; we read his reports on standard weights, measures, and coinage, written while Secretary of State in his capacity as commissioner of the patent system; we note how nearly every trip, ostensibly for pleasure and relaxation, was put to some genuinely practical use—the collection of particular strains of rice, the effort to eradicate the Hessian fly, or the investigation of viniculture. As the Marquis de Chastellux wrote in 1782: "It seemed as if from his youth he had placed his mind, as he had done his house, on an elevated situation, from which he might contemplate the universe."

This breadth is nowhere more eloquently evidenced than in Jefferson's lifelong love of books. This could be —and has been[5]—the subject of considerable study and discussion; let us note here only that Thomas Jefferson built three separate libraries, each more impressive than

5 See, for example, the essay by Arthur Bestor on "Thomas Jefferson and the Freedom of Books," in Arthur Bestor, David C. Mearns, and Jonathan Daniels, *Three Presidents and Their Books* (Urbana, Ill.: University of Illinois Press, 1955).

its predecessor, and each among the very finest in the land at the time. A fire at his home at Shadwell in 1770 destroyed his entire early collection. This he immediately set about skillfully and effectively to replace. So much so that, in 1815, after the British burning of Washington, Jefferson's private library, which with over six thousand volumes was more than twice the size of the lost government collection, became the nucleus for the new National Library of Congress. A third library was laboriously collected and was intended for the University of Virginia, but the insolvency of Jefferson's estate at his death meant that this hope was frustrated. The catholicity of these libraries and of Jefferson's bibliophilia was strikingly indicated as, in June 1825, he sent to a Boston bookseller a listing of over three thousand titles of those works, in nearly every field of learning, which he thought were needed for the library of the university.

The interpretation of any great writing is enhanced by some perception of the character or the temperament of the writer. Of course, the magnitude of Jefferson's impact is in part to be explained by the happy combination of vast energy and industry with a long and unusually healthy life. (It is reported that at his death, copies of some twenty-six thousand of his letters were found filed at Monticello, and Julian Boyd estimates that Jefferson's total correspondence numbered over fifty thousand distinct writings.) Clearly, too, his life and his writing indicate patience, self-discipline, and quiet confidence of a very high order. More pertinent, however, and less susceptible of facile summary were certain fundamental paradoxes in the Jeffersonian outlook, paradoxes but not necessarily contradictions, which are certainly evident in his discussions of education. There is, in the first place, the contrast in Jefferson between innovative and experimental inclinations on the one hand, and adherence to certain clear-cut orthodoxies on the other. In the second place, Jefferson, for all the democratic (though he rarely used the word) convictions he expressed, never lost touch with either his aristocratic origins or his belief in the need for the excellence which only cultivation of the "natural aristocracy of talents and virtues" brings. In the third place, Jefferson is certainly one of the most exquisite illustrations of the proposition that theory is the most practical of man's instruments; seldom has one whose theoretical vision leaps so high remained so immersed in the most mundane utilitarian concerns. In the fourth place, and closely allied with this last, is the remarkable fusion of the aesthetic and the scientific in Jefferson; artist and engineer, mathematician and dirt-farmer, political philosopher and practicing politician all join and are somehow accommodated in the one person. This is not a character to be explained, but surely it is one we can appreciate. Once, while on a brief holiday sojourn at Monticello during his term as Secretary of State, he wrote his close friend, the eminent astronomer, David Rittenhouse: "I am here indulging in reverie and rural occupations, scarcely permitting anything to occupy my mind seriously. When I count the days I still have to remain here, I wish I could see at their end only the pleasure of meeting you again, and keep behind the curtain the table piled with papers, and the eternal sound of the door bell."[6] Yet, within three years of his "retirement" to Monticello in January 1794, he was elected to the vice-presidency and willingly accepted the return to public life. Here, too, a strange combination: the intense love of rural quiet and agrarian simplicity coupled with an insatiable interest in and zest for the significant work of the world.

As we turn in this volume to a few of Jefferson's writings, we should pay tribute to his skill as a penman and sketch the extent of his written works. All his writing, whether public or private, stands as illustration of his artistry with the written word, and no one familiar with the American Declaration of Independence needs to be shown more to validate the claim. Written when Jefferson was thirty-three, the Declaration dramatically stood as both a consummately expressed philosophy of politics

[6] August 12, 1792, Jefferson Papers, Library of Congress, 13305, as quoted in Malone, op. cit., 2:458.

and morality and a thrilling call to arms.[7] But, beyond
this and his voluminous correspondence, we must note
a few of his other writings, many of which bear directly
upon the history of education in the United States and
from which several of the selections in this anthology are
drawn.

Jefferson prepared (in 1774) *A Summary Statement of
the Rights of British America,* a stirring pronouncement
of the Colonial case against the Crown and a clear
precursor of the libertarian sentiments of the Declaration of Independence. Jefferson wrote a treatise (his only
published "book") on his native state, *Notes on the State
of Virginia* (1781; published in 1785), which contains
extended discussions of his plans and ambitions for education. He prepared much of the *Report of the Committee of Revisors Appointed by the General Assembly of
Virginia in 1776,* a committee charged with recommending to the legislature the changes in the government
necessitated by independence. These "revisals" included
explicit proposals for a common school system, for the
reform of the College of William and Mary, and for the
establishment of an institution to promote scholarship
and research (a "public library and gallery"). Out of a
host of reports, official messages, and drafted opinions,
other than those reprinted in the present volume, special
mention should be made of Jefferson's *Reports of the
Committee* [of the federal Congress] *on the Government
of the Western Territory* (March 1 and 22, 1784) and of
his *Essay on Anglo-Saxon,* eventually published in 1851.
The former provided many of the essentials of the Ordi-
nances of 1785 and 1787, enactments which, like Jefferson
himself, further wedded the democratic state to the public
school. The latter work is eloquent testimony to Jefferson's scholarly interests and attainments. These were, of
course, legion, but in the field of philology he was clearly

[7] The Declaration of Independence is examined with great care
and eloquence by Carl L. Becker in *The Declaration of Independence: A Study in the History of Political Ideas* (New York: Knopf,
1942, and Vintage Books, 1958). Among other attributes, this volume contains copies of the several drafts of the Declaration which
preceded that officially adopted by the Congress.

outstanding. The *Essay* represents and reflects a lifelong effort to promote the study of the origins and development of the English language. This he deemed a fundamental requirement of a complete education.

II

There is no grasping the Jeffersonian educational ideas in their fullness without first sensing the essence of Jeffersonianism as a philosophy of politics, morality, and human destiny. For the realization of the political, moral, and ethical ideals of Jefferson's faith was utterly dependent upon enlightenment and education—and the nature of that education was determined by the demands and challenges of those ideals.

Jefferson believed in enlightenment—he was himself a luminous exemplar of "the Enlightenment," that explosive devotion to the realm of the intellect which gripped most of the Western world during the eighteenth century.[8] Many authorities seem to regard Jefferson as essentially little more than an American outpost of the philosophical rationalism of prerevolutionary France and attribute most of his ideas and convictions to French sources.[9] Jefferson was much more than this. It has been said of him that he was unique among Americans of his day in being truly at home in both worlds: the Old and the New. But the traffic he bore may well have been far more significantly from America to Europe than in the reverse direction; there is considerable evidence to suggest that, in his intellectual dealings with French acquaintances, Jefferson was far more the influential than the influenced party. In a manner not precisely definable, Jefferson was at one and the same time remote from, yet

[8] For valuable discussions of the enlightenment milieu and its philosophical temper, see Carl L. Becker, *The Heavenly City of the Eighteenth Century Philosophers* (New Haven, Conn.: Yale University Press, 1932 and 1959), and Ralph Barton Perry, *Puritanism and Democracy* (New York: Vanguard, 1944), Chapters 6–8, 15–20.

[9] See, for example, Allen O. Hansen, *Liberalism and American Education in the Eighteenth Century* (New York: Macmillan, 1926).

clearly a part of, the mainstreams of the Age of Reason.

The basic ingredient in Jefferson's philosophy is a conception of God. In his own day, and frequently still, Jefferson was characterized as a religious skeptic or an atheist. Occasionally, of course, such designations were assigned for ulterior partisan reasons, though some sincere interpreters of his opinions have found these appraisals accurate. There is a sense, to be sure, in which Jefferson's impatience with sect or dogma or cant often made him seem antireligious and unreservedly secular in outlook. But such a view belies the facts.

For Jefferson believed profoundly in a God and worshipped at His shrine throughout his life. Jefferson's God was essentially the God of "the Enlightenment," the master mind, the supreme artificer, the Creator. This earth, and the creatures that inhabit it, were, for Jefferson, all eloquent manifestations of the indescribable power and skill of God. Natural and human history were unquestionable demonstrations of God's infinite wisdom and all-seeing insight. Social progress was but the inevitable working out of the divine plan—or rather the divine mechanism—set in motion at the creation, with beneficent intent, by this holy Author of Nature.

"All men are endowed by their Creator with certain inalienable rights, and among these rights are . . . liberty. . . ."[10] Jefferson's conception of God required complete disavowal of the possibility that men were differentially endowed with the essence of manhood. To hold that some men possessed, or could legitimately claim, more basic rights or privileges than others was to attribute to God a whimsicality or capriciousness wholly inconsistent with the image of a supreme intelligence. An ordered cosmos, on the contrary, presumed a definite ordered concept of the human nature by which that cosmos would be known, understood, and progressively

[10] In discussing the practice of slavery in *Notes on the State of Virginia* (Query XVIII: The particular customs and manners that may happen to be received in that State), Jefferson asked "can the liberties of a nation be thought secure when we have removed their only firm basis, a conviction in the minds of the people that these liberties are of the gift of God?" (Ford, 3:267).

realized. It followed, therefore, for Jefferson that the nature of man was an essence, bestowed upon man as man by God at creation—and that infringement of that essence was a crime against God as well as man. Human liberties, as proclaimed in the Declaration of Independence, thus stood as God-given attributes and frustration of their fullest expression would be tantamount to opposing the will of God.[11]

Some have contended that it is inaccurate to call Jefferson's faith "deism" and have argued that Thomas Paine's term—the "Religion of Humanity"—is more appropriate.[12] Probably it is still more accurate to speak of Jefferson as a believer in a "deistic humanism," for it

[11] In the course of an extended discussion of liberty and the rights of man, contained in a letter to the French savant, P. S. Du Pont de Nemours, Jefferson wrote:

> I believe with you that morality, compassion, generosity are innate elements of the human constitution; that there exists a right independent of force; that a right to property is founded in our natural wants, in the means with which we are endowed to satisfy these wants, and the right to what we acquire by those means without violating the similar rights of other sensible beings; that no one has a right to obstruct another, exercising his faculties innocently for the relief of sensibilities made a part of his nature; that justice is the fundamental law of society; that the majority, oppressing an individual, is guilty of a crime, abuses its strength, and by acting on the law of the strongest breaks up the foundations of society; that action by the citizens in person, in affairs within their reach and competence, and in all others by representatives, chosen immediately, and removable by themselves, constitutes the essence of a republic; that all governments are more or less republican in proportion as this principle enters more or less into their composition; and that a government by representation is capable of extension over a greater surface of country than one of any other form.

This but augments the principle, declared in his famous letter to Madison regarding the proposed new constitution for the American states, almost thirty years before, that "a bill of rights is what the people are entitled to against every government on earth, general or particular, and what no just government should refuse, or rest on inference." (Letter to de Nemours, April 24, 1816, Ford, 10:24; letter to Madison, December 20, 1787, Boyd, 12:440; see also the present volume, pp. 32–38, for letter to Madison.)

[12] Daniel J. Boorstin, The Lost World of Thomas Jefferson (New York: Henry Holt, 1948, or Boston: Beacon Press, 1960), p. 156.

is crystal-clear that he regarded man as, in some sense at
least, a child of God, and he found that God to be rational and purposeful. But was Jefferson a "Christian"?
Not, certainly, in the sense of orthodox belief in the
divinity of Christ or the supernatural inspiration of the
Bible. Yet he frequently and at times vigorously declared
his allegiance to the Christian ethic and proclaimed that
Christ was the greatest teacher of morality in history.

For Jefferson, as we have seen, man's possession of
God-given natural rights was neither partial nor conditional; it was absolute. "Nothing is unchangeable but
the inherent and unalienable rights of man," Jefferson
wrote near the end of his long life[13]—and by the inner
logic of this doctrine, such rights could not be conceived
except as *equally* the possession of all. Thus, a fundamental corollary to the foregoing principles—and one
with vast significance for the conduct of education—was
commitment to the provision of equal opportunity. Inherent identity in essence required full freedom to develop as far as capacity allowed.

Rights in equal measure—but potential and ability in
vastly varying degrees. Jefferson never lost his central
concern for the fullest possible development of the
minds and skills of all men. But of almost equal importance in his eyes was the nurture and encouragement of
the "natural aristocracy of virtue and talents," for it was
to this small group that mankind must look for the protection of those precious universal prerogatives and for

This is a provocative, though occasionally debatable, discussion of
the metaphysical assumptions and cosmological convictions of the
Jeffersonian generation. It is particularly useful as providing insight
into the conceptions of the physical world which accompanied the
Jeffersonian approach to morality and politics. But for an examination of the ideas and outlook of Thomas Jefferson alone, the most
incisive and illuminating treatment to date is that of Adrienne
Koch, *The Philosophy of Thomas Jefferson* (New York: Columbia
University Press, 1943). Separate chapters deal in turn with Jefferson's attitudes and convictions in a variety of fields, including politics, morals, religion, human nature, and education.

13 Letter to Major John Cartwright, June 5, 1824 (Washington,
7:359).

leadership in advancing human welfare. So it is that the Jeffersonian proposals for education, from the famous Bill for the More General Diffusion of Knowledge of 1779 to the plans for the University of Virginia in 1818 and after, never seem to be out of touch with the needs of both groups: the public and its leaders.

As man came more fully to recognize and appreciate his essential humanity—his rights and liberties—it followed for Jefferson that man's conception of his nature and his life's role would develop and change. Of necessity, the very framework and circumstances of his life would be altered. The fulfillment of human destiny, therefore of the divine purpose for man, involved a process of continual development, of ceaseless change. Change, then, was to be welcomed, prepared for, indeed sought after. Writing to James Madison in 1789, Jefferson maintained that "the earth belongs in usufruct to the living . . . the dead have neither powers nor rights over it."[14] Thus, no generation has any authority to bind or commit its successors; even laws and constitutions must be seen as subject to reconsideration and revision. Believing this, says Dumas Malone, "he could be no idolater of any constitution. His genius was not merely that of freedom and reasonableness. It was also the genius of experiment and change."[15]

Experiment and change thus become the signs and agencies of the fulfillment of the divine purpose for man. To block or thwart such development or innovation, especially in the name or interests of tradition, the status quo, or custom, was anathema to Jefferson. It was his fundamental conviction that each living generation must be free and autonomous that led him to propose the legitimacy of revolution.[16] "Rebellion to tyrants is obedience to God." Only as men were free to think, test, decide for themselves were they behaving truly as men

14 September 6, 1789 (Ford, 5:116).
15 Malone, *op. cit.*, 2:179.
16 See the letter to W. S. Smith, November 13, 1787 (Boyd, 12:356–57). "The tree of liberty must be refreshed from time to time with the blood of patriots and tyrants."

"endowed by their Creator." God had granted these natural liberties to man *in order that* His purpose would be achieved and resistance to restrictions upon these liberties thus received divine sanction. In the words of Clinton Rossiter, "man without liberty was a contradiction in terms."[17]

What are the instruments of legitimate change, the means of ensuring that change will truly be *progress?* Here again Jefferson is clearly to be seen as an authentic example of the eighteenth-century Enlightenment. Change is progress, innovation is advance only as it proceeds from a base which is built of the largest possible background of genuine experience, the fullest application of available evidence, and the freest range for the play of reason over all. Once, Jefferson remarked that he considered Bacon, Locke, and Newton "as the three greatest men that have ever lived, without any exception, and as having laid the foundation of those superstructures which have been raised in the Physical and Moral Sciences. . . ."[18] To be sure, some will find that this simply seems to reinforce their assessment of Jefferson as atheistic. Others will see in this evidence of the lesser place he sometimes seems to have assigned to the humanistic sphere. The statement is far more revealing, however, of his central devotion to the rational, scientific, pragmatic approach to knowledge and truth—and for him, therefore, a free society's pre-eminent commitment must be to the support of those principles and institutions which respect and enhance that rational process.

These principles constitute the backbone of Jefferson's political philosophy, and he spent most of his life attempting to outline and promote institutions appropriate to these principles. It is, of course, true, as Merrill D. Peterson has skillfully pointed out, that "His

[17] Clinton Rossiter, *Seedtime of the Republic: The Origin of the American Tradition of Political Liberty* (New York: Harcourt, Brace, 1953), p. 377. This provides a superb discussion of the roots of the Jeffersonian political philosophy.

[18] Letter to John Trumbull, February 15, 1788 (Boyd, 14:561).

speculative and practical sides were frequently confused.
Few men took into account that Jefferson's private self,
as expressed in his letters, might not coincide with his
public self. Or that his opinion at one time might not
represent his opinion under different circumstances. Or
that a man of his intellectual temperament did not often
bother to qualify felicitous generalizations."[19] The in-
consistencies and contradictions one finds in Jefferson,
however, do not alter essentially the fundamental political ideals he adored nor the outlines of the major institutions he believed would further those ideals.

No political theory, however detached or speculative,
ever ranges in perfect symmetry over all great questions of power, organization, and obedience. The political theorist concentrates inevitably upon the problems of his own civilization . . . 'the felt necessities' of
the age. . . . The political theorists of the Revolution
were no exception to this rule. Heirs of a great tradition of personal liberty, children of an age concerned
with the individual rather than the community, targets
of a policy that seemed to defy the dictates of abstract
justice, they used up most of their energy defining the
rights of man and devising methods of protecting
them.[20]

Popular government, popular controls, and a constitution for the maintenance of popular rights and responsi-
bilities: These were for him the critical essentials of a
genuinely republican political order.

In 1774, Jefferson drafted a set of resolutions intended
as instructions to Virginia's delegates to the first Continental Congress. Though never officially considered by
the House of Burgesses, his remarks appeared as a
pamphlet (not authorized by him) entitled *A Summary*

19 Merrill D. Peterson, *The Jefferson Image in the American
Mind* (New York: Oxford University Press, 1960), p. 64. This is an
incisive and revealing study of the nature and the significance of
Jefferson as a philosophical and political symbol in American history.

20 Rossiter, *op. cit.,* p. 375.

View of the Rights of British America, in which the
political principles which guided his entire life are em-
bodied. Here, in what was his first published statement,
Jefferson called upon the King to reflect "that he is no
more than the chief officer of the people, appointed by
the laws, and circumscribed with definite powers, to
assist in working the great machine of government
erected for their use, and consequently subject to their
superintendence." Jefferson chose to remind the King
that the colonials possessed the right, "which nature has
given to all men," of "establishing new societies, under
such laws and regulations as to them shall seem most
likely to promote public happiness. . . . From the nature
of things, every society must at all times possess within
itself the sovereign powers of legislation."[21]

Three years before his death, he wrote at length to an
eminent Greek visitor (at the time of the struggle in
Greece, circa 1820, to secure independence from Turkey).
The letter is a compelling discussion of these same political convictions, stressing natural rights and liberties, representative popular government, regular and frequent
elections, a constitutional foundation with explicit provision for amendment, and systematic attention to public
education. The letter concludes with an eloquent yet
succinct summary of those "principles in which all agree,
and which all cherish as vitally essential to the protection
of the life, liberty, property, and safety of the citizen.

"1. Freedom of religion, restricted only from acts of
trespass on that of others.

"2. Freedom of person, securing every one from imprisonment, or other bodily restraint, but by the laws of
the land. This is effected by the well-known law of
habeas corpus.

"3. Trial by jury, the best of all safeguards for the
person, the property, and the fame of every individual.

21 As quoted in Edward Dumbauld, ed., *The Political Writings
of Thomas Jefferson—Representative Selections* (New York: Liberal
Arts Press, 1955), pp. 16–17, 29. This is an excellent collection of
Jefferson's pronouncements in the political realm, introduced by a
very helpful essay on Jefferson's political ideals and activities.

"4. The exclusive right of legislation and taxation in the representatives of the people.

"5. Freedom of the press, subject only to liability for personal injuries. This formidable censor of the public functionaries, by arraigning them at the tribunal of public opinion, produces reform peaceably, which must otherwise be done by revolution. It is also the best instrument for enlightening the mind of man, and improving him as a rational, moral, and social being." [22]

Throughout his writings, Jefferson made abundantly evident his conviction that the crucial element in any society based upon liberty and law is enlightenment. It may perhaps be questioned whether he regarded organized education or an untrammeled press as the primary element in the promotion of intelligent freedom, but the question loses significance as we recognize his call for both. "The basis of our governments being the opinion of the people, the very first object should be to keep that right; and were it left to me to decide whether we should have a government without newspapers, or newspapers without a government, I should not hesitate a moment to prefer the latter. But I should mean that every man should receive those papers & be capable of reading them." [23]

For Jefferson, then, the healthy, sturdy, progressive, free society can be built only on a foundation of popular intelligence. "I know no safe depository of the ultimate powers of the society but the people themselves; and if we think them not enlightened enough to exercise their control with a wholesome discretion, the remedy is not to take it from them, but to inform their discretion by education." [24] Freedom and science, liberty and literacy are reciprocally and inextricably interdependent; the agencies and instruments for the cultivation of literacy and the advancement of science stand with the legisla-

22 Letter to M. Adamantios Coray, October 31, 1823 (Lipscomb and Bergh, 15:489).
23 Letter to Edward Carrington, January 16, 1787 (Boyd, 11:49); see also the present volume, pp. 101–03.
24 Letter to William C. Jarvis, September 28, 1820 (Ford, 10:161).

ture and the courts as absolutely essential to the welfare of the republic. School and college thus become, in a manner and to a degree not heretofore conceived in Western civilization, the most vital pillars of human happiness and security. It is hardly surprising that in Jefferson America finds one of its most persuasive and significant educational philosophers.

III

The Jeffersonian discussions of education bear out and reflect the endeavor to apply the moral-ethical and socio-political principles which Jefferson so unfailingly espoused.[25] The selections to follow provide many of the particulars of the Jeffersonian conception of the education appropriate to a free people. Let us here simply suggest certain of the general propositions by which this conception was governed. "If a nation expects to be ignorant and free, in a state of civilization," wrote Jef-

[25] The place of Thomas Jefferson in the history of American education has been dealt with most extensively in Roy J. Honeywell, *The Educational Work of Thomas Jefferson* (Cambridge, Mass.: Harvard University Press, 1931). This excellent scholarly monograph is supplemented by a full bibliography and a series of appendices reproducing several of the major Jeffersonian statements on education. Somewhat analogous in intent, though much less thorough, is Charles F. Arrowood, *Thomas Jefferson and Education in a Republic* (New York: McGraw-Hill, 1930). See also the chapter on Jefferson in Robert Ulich, *History of Educational Thought* (New York: American Book, 1945); Chapter 20, "Church and School," in Malone, *op. cit.*, Vol. I; and Chapters 11 and 12 in Caleb P. Patterson, *The Constitutional Principles of Thomas Jefferson* (Austin, Texas: University of Texas Press, 1953).

The founding of the University of Virginia and Jefferson's place in that history have been treated most extensively in John S. Patton, *Jefferson, Cabell, and the University of Virginia* (New York: Neale, 1906) and in Philip A. Bruce, *History of the University of Virginia, 1819-1919*, Vol. I (New York: Macmillan, 1920). The entire episode is more succinctly, yet most effectively reported in Honeywell, *op. cit.*

For Jefferson's role in the struggle for separation of church and state, examined with particular reference to the conduct of public education, see R. F. Butts, *The American Tradition in Religion and Education* (Boston: Beacon Press, 1950) and James M. O'Neill, *Religion and Education Under the Constitution* (New York: Harper, 1949).

ferson in 1816, "it expects what never was and never will be."[26] This famous dictum was but the reiteration of his never-failing belief in the dependence of representative government upon popular enlightenment. Thirty years before, in a letter to George Washington, he had declared that "It is an axiom in my mind that our liberty can never be safe but in the hands of the people themselves, and that too of the people with a certain degree of instruction. This it is the business of the state to effect, and on a general plan."[27] And moreover, "the qualifications for self-government are not innate. They are the result of habit and long training."[28]

Of what, then, does the state's educational obligation consist? For Jefferson, first and foremost, the state's responsibility was to supply and maintain a "system of general instruction, which shall reach every description of our citizens, from the richest to the poorest"—a system of public education dedicated to the cultivation of intelligent citizenship and to the identification and training of responsible leadership. Necessarily, this obligation was seen as one of providing educational opportunities which did no violence to the essence of man, which guaranteed each the chance to advance to the limit of his powers.

Thus, the central focus was the promotion of the life of freedom, the free man in a free society. Man, Jefferson believed, is most free when he is most nearly or completely self-sufficient, hence his education must be concerned with developing such inner resourcefulness. And this, for him, was primarily, though not exclusively, an intellectual matter. In his delightful letter to Mrs. Maria Cosway, the remarkable dialogue between his Head and his Heart, Jefferson had his Head say: "The art of life is the art of avoiding pain. . . . The most effectual means of being secure against pain is to retire within ourselves and to suffice for our own happiness. Those, which depend on ourselves, are the only pleasures a wise man

26 Letter to Col. Charles Yancey, January 6, 1816 (Ford, 10:4).
27 January 4, 1786 (Boyd, 9:151).
28 Letter to Edward Everett, March 27, 1824 (Lipscomb and Bergh, 16:22).

will count on: for nothing is ours which another may
deprive us of. Hence the inestimable value of the intellectual pleasures."[29] The interdependence of this conviction with his ideas of the good society is clear, for
Jefferson firmly believed that society encouraged or
fostered such self-sufficiency to the degree that it was
basically rural, agrarian, close to nature and the land. As
he wrote in the *Notes on the State of Virginia,* "Those
who labor in the earth are the chosen people of God, if
ever he had a chosen people, whose breasts he has made
his peculiar deposit for substantial and genuine virtue."[30] This outlook led, in turn, to the insistence upon
limited, explicitly constitutional government as the
policy most conducive to freedom so conceived and the
good society so defined.

But this intellectualism, for Jefferson, was not fruitful
in isolation. Hence it is coupled in all his thinking with
a very strong current of utilitarianism. Man, he thought,
is freest, hence most man-like, when he is engaged in
truly useful pursuits, working in ways which demonstra-
bly contribute to human betterment. "I am not fond of
reading what is merely abstract and unapplied immediately to some useful science," he wrote. As before, such
beneficent utilitarianism was possible in Jefferson's view
to the extent that social and political institutions were
kept small, intimate, local, or decentralized. It may be
partially correct to cite Jefferson as a pre-eminent ex-
ponent of a kind of practical humanism which has come
to be the hallmark of much of modern American education. But it is far more accurate and important to see
that education as conceived by Jefferson—if it is not to
become the vehicle of indoctrination, exploitation, or en-
slavement—must be directed toward the development of
inner resourcefulness and social utility.

This juxtaposition of the philosophical and the utilitarian suggests that Jefferson would regard as empty and
meaningless the recurrent discussions of "liberal" *versus*
"vocational" education. Any attempt to separate the two

29 October 12, 1786 (Boyd, 9:448-49).
30 *Notes on the State of Virginia,* as in Ford, 3:268.

would seem to him both fruitless and foolhardy, for his conception of the free man and the good society clearly assumed a necessary, indeed an inescapable, synthesis of these two elements. Jefferson was like the Greeks in holding citizenship as man's chief vocation and preparation for that citizenship as society's chief concern. Thus the Jeffersonian "curriculum" is essentially political in its nature, hence basically philosophical, while it is civic and social in its aims, hence fundamentally utilitarian. Seldom have the two been so skillfully blended in the discussion of education.

Of what did this curriculum consist? Again, the details are supplied in the readings which follow but a few introductory generalizations may be appropriate. The primary concern was to train up "free" men, men who could think and act independently of pressure or propaganda. When Jefferson wrote of the "general diffusion of knowledge," this was not a call for the seven liberal arts or for a broad exposure to culture for the masses. Rather, in his proposals for universal schooling, Jefferson was concerned to supply all persons with the basic *tools* of intelligent citizenship, and with the means whereby they could carry on their own education throughout life. Fundamental to everything, Jefferson felt, was language, the ability to read, write, and speak in one's native tongue. Hence, the primary or common school was seen as an agency dedicated almost exclusively to the development of this facility.

The function of the university, in Jefferson's eyes, was that of training men for the particular professions of law, medicine, or engineering, and for scientific pursuits —and of preparing them to assume positions of leadership in society. These departments depend upon certain linguistic and mathematical tools beyond the requirements of universal education; these prerequisites—the classical and certain of the modern foreign languages, along with elementary mathematics—he regarded as the responsibility of the "schools of intermediate grade." Governing Jefferson's view of both primary and secondary schooling was his sense that the most effective learning up to the age of fifteen or sixteen is memoriter learning, and that mastery of the basic processes of language and mathematics is essentially a matter of practice and habituation.

In a sense, all of this—from rudimentary language in the village school to advanced chemistry at the university —was preliminary or subsidiary in Jefferson's educational thinking. The ideal was not a merely skillful man —it was a thoughtful and responsible man. Possessed of the basic skills, Jefferson believed such a man was equipped to move into almost any realm *on his own*. Thus it is that what the modern calls "independent study," but on a lifelong plan, was perhaps Jefferson's cardinal pedagogical principle. The most important branch, once one has mastered the disciplines, is history, and the list of books Jefferson was so ready to supply to those seeking his educational advice usually included more works in that field than in any other. Yet even here, as he wrote to his nephew, Thomas Mann Randolph, "you can proceed by yourself in a regular series of historical reading. . . . History need not be hurried, but may give way to the other sciences; because history can be pursued after you shall have left your present situation, as well as while you remain in it."[31]

Jefferson's stress on history was couched, however, in a conception of learning which reflected the catholicity of his own tastes. Conceding that everyone must concentrate his energies in a certain direction, he nevertheless held that most men could, and that all men destined for leadership should, be at least conversant with the several intellectual departments. The original specifications for the University of Virginia provided for ten professorships embracing the fields of ancient and modern languages, natural and physical sciences, politics, law, and literature. But, given a common basic education, Jefferson was vigorous in his rejection of the idea of a standard university course for all students.

31 August 27, 1786 (Boyd, 9:306–07); *see also* the present volume, pp. 140–44.

I am not fully informed of the practices at Harvard, but [in the development of the University of Virginia] there is one from which we shall certainly vary, although it has been copied, I believe, by nearly every college and academy in the United States. That is, the holding the students to one prescribed course of reading, and disallowing exclusive application to those branches only which are to qualify them for the particular vocations to which they are destined. We shall, on the contrary, allow them the uncontroled choice in the lectures they shall choose to attend, and require elementary qualification only and sufficient age. Our institution will proceed on the principle of doing all the good it can without consulting its own pride or ambition; of letting every one come and listen to whatever he thinks may improve the condition of his mind.[32]

It is probably incorrect to regard Jefferson as a philosopher of education in any systematic sense. Jefferson's importance for the field of education lies in the ideals he proclaimed for America and in his ringing insistence that without energetic attention to education such ideals are foredoomed. We sense this most fully, of course, as we endeavor to set his thoughts in the full context of our national beginnings, for nothing is more vital to a people than an intelligent awareness of its traditions and their origins. Thus the selections included in this volume deal not alone with Jefferson's explicit comments on education but also with the political and social ideals by which the schools and colleges were to be governed. The American educational tradition is here viewed broadly as including the climate of freedom and tolerance which for Jefferson was so vital; this definition also encompasses something of Jefferson's conception of the manner and character of truly educated men and women. The present collection is not offered as a compendium of everything ever written by

[32] Letter to George Ticknor, July 16, 1823 (Lipscomb and Bergh, 15:455).

Jefferson on the subject of education; neither is it an effort to draw up the metes and bounds of a Jeffersonian school of educational thought. The intent here is rather, by selecting from the incredibly voluminous materials available,[33] to show the major lines of his educational ideas and to suggest something of the continuing significance of those ideas for modern education.

IV

And wherein lies that continuing significance? Why is it not only appropriate but genuinely vital that we re-examine the Jeffersonian educational literature in the second half of the twentieth century? Let it be suggested that Jefferson's continuing relevance can be said to rest on three levels. He is, in the first place, refreshingly and uncommonly cogent as he discusses a number of specific pedagogical questions for which we have yet to find altogether acceptable answers. The education of the gifted, the management and dispensation of scholarships, the proper allocation of responsibility for educational support and control—these and many more problems of constantly recurring importance are considered with calm and wisdom. To be sure, we, with our modern perspective and experience, are not led to an automatic acceptance of Jeffersonian dicta simply because of their authorship, and, moreover, he had his prejudices and his blind spots. (He was, for example, never able to muster any real interest in geology, and his distaste for fiction was rather strenuously elaborated.) Nevertheless, few discussions of the educational policies appropriate to a representative democracy are more valuable; none, perhaps, match his in idealism.

This leads, in the second place, to the suggestion that

33 The very volume of Jefferson's discussions of education illustrates how endlessly important was that subject to him. Toward the close of his long life he wrote that popular education "as it was the earliest, so will it be the latest of all the public concerns in which I shall permit myself to take an interest." Letter to Joseph C. Cabell, January 14, 1818 (Ford, 10:102).

the relevance of Jefferson is even more profoundly present at the level of intellectual and social goals. No one is
likely to maintain that the ideals set forth in the
Declaration of Independence and continuously throughout Jefferson's writings have lost either their vitality or
their centrality for American civilization. To be sure,
debate never ends as to the means whereby these ideals
are to be approached—in the conduct of education as
in other realms of the national life. But the ideals
themselves, for the life of freedom and for the education
essential to that freedom, are as viable and as sparkling
as ever. Perhaps even more significant, as previously
noted and as the readings demonstrate, Jefferson married
these ideals with action, he worked constantly to clothe
them with the flesh of concrete applicability. It is in
this sense particularly that the Jeffersonian message has
validity and inspiration far beyond the boundaries of
the United States.[34] For, as other peoples and nations
struggle to achieve some measure of the freedom to
which, as Jefferson saw, all men aspire, the logic and
the reasonableness of his principles assume a world-wide
significance. Probably no American has spoken with such
clarity to men everywhere in their quest for dignity
and happiness. In this sense, Jefferson's discussions of
education, anachronistic though they may be at certain
points, are among the most important proposals ever
made for the realization of democratic ideals on a universal plane.

But, in the third place, Jefferson on education may be
even more important as a source of ideas or guidance in
the determination of educational policy for the future.
As the United States Supreme Court has repeatedly
pointed out in recent years, national policy can be
wisely developed only as we refer intelligently to the climate of opinion which was the context for the enunci-

34 Jefferson was himself well aware of the global potential lying
within the ideas he was propounding. See, for example, his letters
to: P. S. Du Pont de Nemours, April 24, 1816 (Ford, 10:22–25); The
Chevalier de Onis, April 28, 1814 (Washington, 6:342); and Lafa-
yette, May 14, 1817 (Ford, 10:82–86).

ation of our guiding ideals and the formulation of our
basic law. Jefferson can safely be said to have been the
outstanding personage among the founding fathers for
interest in and devotion to the educational process, as he
was the most articulate, incisive champion of intellectual
and political liberty. As such, in a time when the importance of systematic universal education is more widely and
energetically accepted than ever before, and when the
ideals of freedom are challenged as never before, his
educational principles, dedicated to the advancement
of a democratic political order, demand the most serious
attention. Some words addressed to the president of
Harvard University carry Jefferson's charge across two
centuries and constitute a challenge to American education in any age. "It is for such institutions as that
over which you preside so worthily, Sir, to do justice
to our country, it's productions, and it's genius. It is
the work to which the young men, whom you are
forming, should lay their hands. We have spent the
prime of our lives in procuring them the precious
blessing of liberty. Let them spend theirs in shewing
that it is the great parent of science and of virtue; and
that a nation will be great in both always in proportion
as it is free."[35]

[35] Letter to Joseph Willard, March 24, 1789 (Boyd, 14:699).

1: The Precious Blessing of Liberty

"Freedom, the first-born daughter of science."

It is not only fitting, it is inescapable that an examination of Thomas Jefferson's educational views open with a consideration of his unequivocal commitment to human liberty. In the intellectual sphere, one expresses this principle in terms of "academic freedom" and for Jefferson, as free government depends upon education, so is academic freedom the indispensable condition of genuine education. This central commitment to liberty was evident throughout Jefferson's long and fruitful life, though nowhere more lucidly than in the well-known words of the Declaration of Independence, which statement, as he noted long afterwards, was intended simply "to place before mankind the common sense of the subject. . . ."

Liberty and the unalienable rights of man were uppermost in his thoughts when he commented, as for example in the letters from Paris to James Madison and Francis Hopkinson here reproduced, upon the proposed new constitution for the United States. His uncompromising hostility to any restrictions upon freedom of expression and publication was probably nowhere more dramatically displayed than in the resolutions he drafted (secretly) for the consideration of the Kentucky legislature in protest against the Alien and Sedition Laws of 1798. His fundamental insistence in this statement that government should be limited and decentralized—leading, among other things, to his steadfast adherence to the principle of local responsibility for public general education—stemmed directly from his anxieties for human freedom and his determination to guard it from violation.

27

Three years later, on the occasion of his first inauguration to the presidency, Jefferson, despite one of the bitterest, most vicious political battles in American history, could nevertheless proclaim that "if there be any among us who would wish to dissolve this Union or to change its republican form, let them stand undisturbed as monuments of the safety with which error of opinion may be tolerated where reason is left free to combat it." This note is rarely absent from the Jefferson writings; the letters to Thomas Seymour and Nicholas Dufief are but two from scores that might be cited enlarging upon the same all-important theme.

SEE ALSO:

Letter to Archibald Stuart, December 23, 1791 (Ford, 5:408–11).

Letter to M. D'Ivernois, February 6, 1795 (Ford, 7:2–6).

Letter to Benjamin Rush, September 3, 1800 (Ford, 7:458–61).

Letter to Henri Gregoire, February 25, 1809 (Ford, 9:246–47).

Letter to Joseph C. Cabell, February 2, 1816 (Koch-Peden, 660).

Letter to Samuel Kercheval, July 12, 1816 (Ford, 10:37–46).

THE DECLARATION OF INDEPENDENCE AS ADOPTED BY CONGRESS*

IN CONGRESS, JULY 4, 1776.

THE UNANIMOUS DECLARATION

OF THE THIRTEEN UNITED STATES

OF AMERICA,

When in the Course of human events, it becomes necessary for one people to dissolve the political bands which have connected them with another, and to assume

* Julian P. Boyd, ed., *The Papers of Thomas Jefferson* (Princeton, N. J.: Princeton University Press, 1950 *et seq.*), 1:429–32.

among the powers of the earth, the separate and equal station to which the Laws of Nature and of Nature's God entitle them, a decent respect to the opinions of mankind requires that they should declare the causes which impel them to the separation. We hold these truths to be self-evident, that all men are created equal, that they are endowed by their Creator with certain unalienable Rights, that among these are Life, Liberty and the pursuit of Happiness. That to secure these rights, Governments are instituted among Men, deriving their just powers from the consent of the governed, That whenever any Form of Government becomes destructive of these ends, it is the Right of the People to alter or to abolish it, and to institute new Government, laying its foundation on such principles and organizing its powers in such form, as to them shall seem most likely to effect their Safety and Happiness. Prudence, indeed, will dictate that Governments long established should not be changed for light and transient causes; and accordingly all experience hath shewn, that mankind are more disposed to suffer, while evils are sufferable, than to right themselves by abolishing the forms to which they are accustomed. But when a long train of abuses and usurpations, pursuing invariably the same Object evinces a design to reduce them under absolute Despotism, it is their right, it is their duty, to throw off such Government, and to provide new Guards for their future security. Such has been the patient sufferance of these Colonies; and such is now the necessity which constrains them to alter their former Systems of Government. The history of the present King of Great Britain is a history of repeated injuries and usurpations, all having in direct object the establishment of an absolute Tyranny over these States. To prove this, let Facts be submitted to a candid world. He has refused his Assent to Laws, the most wholesome and necessary for the public good. He has forbidden his Governors to pass Laws of immediate and pressing importance, unless suspended in their operation till his Assent should be obtained; and when so suspended, he has utterly neglected to attend to them.

He has refused to pass other Laws for the accommodation of large districts of people, unless those people would relinquish the right of Representation in the Legislature, a right inestimable to them and formidable to tyrants only. He has called together legislative bodies at places unusual, uncomfortable, and distant from the depository of their public Records, for the sole purpose of fatiguing them into compliance with his measures. He has dissolved Representative Houses repeatedly, for opposing with manly firmness his invasions on the rights of the people. He has refused for a long time, after such dissolutions, to cause others to be elected; whereby the Legislative powers, incapable of Annihilation, have returned to the People at large for their exercise; the State remaining in the mean time exposed to all the dangers of invasion from without, and convulsions within. He has endeavoured to prevent the population of these States; for that purpose obstructing the Laws for Naturalization of Foreigners; refusing to pass others to encourage their migrations hither, and raising the conditions of new Appropriations of Lands. He has obstructed the Administration of Justice, by refusing his Assent to Laws for establishing Judiciary powers. He has made Judges dependent on his Will alone, for the tenure of their offices, and the amount and payment of their salaries. He has erected a multitude of New Offices, and sent hither swarms of Officers to harrass our people, and eat out their substance. He has kept among us, in times of peace, standing Armies without the Consent of our legislatures. He has affected to render the Military independent of and superior to the Civil power. He has combined with others to subject us to a jurisdiction foreign to our constitution, and unacknowledged by our laws; giving his Assent to their Acts of pretended Legislation: For Quartering large bodies of armed troops among us: For protecting them, by a mock Trial, from punishment for any Murders which they should commit on the Inhabitants of these States: For cutting off our Trade with all parts of the world: For imposing Taxes on us without our Consent: For depriving us in many cases of the benefits of Trial by Jury: For transporting us beyond Seas to be tried for pretended offences: For abolishing the free System of English Laws in a neighbouring Province, establishing therein an Arbitrary government, and enlarging its Boundaries so as to render it at once an example and fit instrument for introducing the same absolute rule into these Colonies: For taking away our Charters, abolishing our most valuable Laws, and altering fundamentally the Forms of our Governments: For suspending our own Legislatures, and declaring themselves invested with power to legislate for us in all cases whatsoever. He has abdicated Government here, by declaring us out of his Protection and waging War against us. He has plundered our seas, ravaged our Coasts, burnt our towns, and destroyed the Lives of our people. He is at this time transporting large Armies of foreign Mercenaries to compleat the works of death, desolation and tyranny, already begun with circumstances of Cruelty & perfidy scarcely paralleled in the most barbarous ages, and totally unworthy the Head of a civilized nation. He has constrained our fellow Citizens taken Captive on the high Seas to bear Arms against their Country, to become the executioners of their friends and Brethren, or to fall themselves by their Hands. He has excited domestic insurrections amongst us, and has endeavoured to bring on the inhabitants of our frontiers, the merciless Indian Savages, whose known rule of warfare, is an undistinguished destruction of all ages, sexes and conditions. In every stage of these Oppressions We have Petitioned for Redress in the most humble terms: Our repeated Petitions have been answered only by repeated injury. A Prince, whose character is thus marked by every act which may define a Tyrant, is unfit to be the ruler of a free people. Nor have We been wanting in attentions to our Brittish brethren. We have warned them from time to time of attempts by their legislature to extend an unwarrantable jurisdiction over us. We have reminded them of the circumstances of our emigration and settle-

ment here. We have appealed to their native justice and
magnanimity, and we have conjured them by the ties
of our common kindred to disavow these usurpations,
which, would inevitably interrupt our connections and
correspondence. They too have been deaf to the voice
of justice and of consanguinity. We must, therefore,
acquiesce in the necessity, which denounces our Separation, and hold them, as we hold the rest of mankind,
Enemies in War, in Peace Friends.

We, therefore, the Representatives of the united States
of America, in General Congress, Assembled, appealing
to the Supreme Judge of the world for the rectitude
of our intentions, do, in the Name, and by Authority
of the good People of these Colonies, solemnly publish
and declare, That these United Colonies are, and
of Right ought to be Free and Independent States; that
they are Absolved from all Allegiance to the British
Crown, and that all political connection between them
and the State of Great Britain, is and ought to be totally
dissolved; and that as Free and Independent States,
they have full Power to levy War, conclude Peace,
contract Alliances, establish Commerce, and to do all
other Acts and Things which Independent States may
of right do. And for the support of this Declaration,
with a firm reliance on the protection of divine Providence, we mutually pledge to each other our Lives, our
Fortunes and our sacred Honor.

John Hancock

Button Gwinnett	Geo. Taylor
Lyman Hall	James Wilson
Geo Walton.	Geo. Ross
Wm. Hooper	Cæsar Rodney
Joseph Hewes,	Geo Read
John Penn	Tho M:Kean
Edward Rutledge.	Wm. Floyd
Thos. Heyward Junr.	Phil. Livingston
Thomas Lynch Junr.	Frans. Lewis
Arthur Middleton	Lewis Morris
Samuel Chase	Richd. Stockton

Wm. Paca
Thos. Stone
Charles Carroll of
    Carrollton
George Wythe
Richard Henry Lee
Th: Jefferson
Benja. Harrison
Thos. Nelson jr.
Francis Lightfoot Lee
Carter Braxton
Robt. Morris
Benjamin Rush
Benja. Franklin
John Morton
Geo Clymer
Jas. Smith.

Jno Witherspoon
Fras. Hopkinson
John Hart
Abra Clark
Josiah Bartlett
Wm: Whipple
Saml. Adams
John Adams
Robt. Treat Paine
Elbridge Gerry
Step. Hopkins
William Ellery
Roger Sherman
Saml. Huntington
Wm. Williams
Oliver Wolcott
Matthew Thornton

TO JAMES MADISON *

DEAR SIR   Paris Dec. 20. 1787.

My last to you was of Oct. 8 by the Count de Moustier.
Yours of July 18. Sep. 6. and Oct. 24. have been suc-
cessively received, yesterday, the day before and three or
four days before that. I have only had time to read the
letters, the printed papers communicated with them, however interesting, being obliged to lie over till I finish my
dispatches for the packet, which dispatches must go from
hence the day after tomorrow. I have much to thank you
for. First and most for the cyphered paragraph respecting
myself. These little informations are very material towards forming my own decisions. I would be glad even
to know when any individual member thinks I have
gone wrong in any instance. If I know myself it would
not excite ill blood in me, while it would assist to guide
my conduct, perhaps to justify it, and to keep me to my
duty, alert. I must thank you too for the information in

* Boyd, 12:438–42.

Thos. Burke's case, tho' you will have found by a subsequent letter that I have asked of you a further investigation of that matter. It is to gratify the lady who is at the head of the Convent wherein my daughters are, and who, by her attachment and attention to them, lays me under great obligations. I shall hope therefore still to receive from you the result of the further enquiries my second letter had asked.—The parcel of rice which you informed me had miscarried accompanied my letter to the Delegates of S. Carolina. Mr. Bourgoin was to be the bearer of both and both were delivered together into the hands of his relation here who introduced him to me, and who at a subsequent moment undertook to convey them to Mr. Bourgoin. This person was an engraver particularly recommended to Dr. Franklin and Mr. Hopkinson. Perhaps he may have mislaid the little parcel of rice among his baggage.—I am much pleased that the sale of Western lands is so successful. I hope they will absorb all the Certificates of our Domestic debt speedily in the first place, and that then offered for cash they will do the same by our foreign one.

The season admitting only of operations in the Cabinet, and these being in a great measure secret, I have little to fill a letter. I will therefore make up the deficiency by adding a few words on the Constitution proposed by our Convention. I like much the general idea of framing a government which should go on of itself peaceably, without needing continual recurrence to the state legislatures. I like the organization of the government into Legislative, Judiciary and Executive. I like the power given the Legislature to levy taxes; and for that reason solely approve of the greater house being chosen by the people directly. For tho' I think a house chosen by them will be very illy qualified to legislate for the Union, for foreign nations &c. yet this evil does not weigh against the good of preserving inviolate the fundamental principle that the people are not to be taxed but by representatives chosen immediately by themselves. I am captivated by the compromise of the opposite claims of the great and little states, of the latter to equal, and the former to proportional influence. I am much pleased too with the substitution of the method of voting by persons, instead of that of voting by states: and I like the negative given to the Executive with a third of either house, though I should have liked it better had the Judiciary been associated for that purpose, or invested with a similar and separate power. There are other good things of less moment. I will now add what I do not like. First the omission of a bill of rights providing clearly and without the aid of sophisms for freedom of religion, freedom of the press, protection against standing armies, restriction against monopolies, the eternal and unremitting force of the habeas corpus laws, and trials by jury in all matters of fact triable by the laws of the land and not by the law of Nations. To say, as Mr. Wilson does that a bill of rights was not necessary because all is reserved in the case of the general government which is not given, while in the particular ones all is given which is not reserved might do for the Audience to whom it was addressed, but is surely gratis dictum, opposed by strong inferences from the body of the instrument, as well as from the omission of the clause of our present confederation which had declared that in express terms. It was a hard conclusion to say because there has been no uniformity among the states as to the cases triable by jury, because some have been so incautious as to abandon this mode of trial, therefore the more prudent states shall be reduced to the same level of calamity. It would have been much more just and wise to have concluded the other way that as most of the states had judiciously preserved this palladium, those who had wandered should be brought back to it, and to have established general right instead of general wrong. Let me add that a bill of rights is what the people are entitled to against every government on earth, general or particular, and what no just government should refuse, or rest on inference. The second feature I dislike, and greatly dislike, is the abandonment in every instance of the necessity of rotation in office, and most particularly in the case of the President. Experience concurs with reason in concluding that the first magistrate will always be re-elected if the constitution permits it. He is then an officer for life. This once observed it becomes of so much consequence to certain nations to have a friend or a foe at the head of our affairs that they will interfere with money and with arms. A Galloman or an Angloman will be supported by the nation he befriends. If once elected, and at a second or third election outvoted by one or two votes, he will pretend false votes, foul play, hold possession of the reins of government, be supported by the states voting for him, especially if they are the central ones lying in a compact body themselves and separating their opponents: and they will be aided by one nation of Europe, while the majority are aided by another. The election of a President of America some years hence will be much more interesting to certain nations of Europe than ever the election of a king of Poland was. Reflect on all the instances in history antient and modern, of elective monarchies, and say if they do not give foundation for my fears, the Roman emperors, the popes, while they were of any importance, the German emperors till they became hereditary in practice, the kings of Poland, the Deys of the Ottoman dependancies. It may be said that if elections are to be attended with these disorders, the seldomer they are renewed the better. But experience shews that the only way to prevent disorder is to render them uninteresting by frequent changes. An incapacity to be elected a second time would have been the only effectual preventative. The power of removing him every fourth year by the vote of the people is a power which will not be exercised. The king of Poland is removeable every day by the Diet, yet he is never removed.—Smaller objections are the Appeal in fact as well as law, and the binding all persons Legislative, Executive and Judiciary by oath to maintain that constitution. I do not pretend to decide what would be the best method of procuring the establishment of the manifold good things in this constitution, and of getting rid of the bad. Whether by adopting it in hopes of future amendment, or, after it has been duly weighed and canvassed by the people, after seeing the parts they generally dislike, and those they generally approve, to say to them 'We see now what you wish. Send together your deputies again, let them frame a constitution for you omitting what you have condemned, and establishing the powers you approve. Even these will be a great addition to the energy of your government.'—At all events I hope you will not be discouraged from other trials, if the present one should fail of it's full effect.—I have thus told you freely what I like and dislike: merely as a matter of curiosity for I know your own judgment has been formed on all these points after having heard every thing which could be urged on them. I own I am not a friend to a very energetic government. It is always oppressive. The late rebellion in Massachusets has given more alarm than I think it should have done. Calculate that one rebellion in 13 states in the course of 11 years, is but one for each state in a century and a half. No country should be so long without one. Nor will any degree of power in the hands of government prevent insurrections. France with all it's despotism, and two or three hundred thousand men always in arms has had three insurrections in the three years I have been here in every one of which greater numbers were engaged than in Massachusets and a great deal more blood was spilt. In Turkey, which Montesquieu supposes more despotic, insurrections are the events of every day. In England, where the hand of power is lighter than here, but heavier than with us they happen every half dozen years. Compare again the ferocious depredations of their insurgents with the order, the moderation and the almost self extinguishment of ours.— After all, it is my principle that the will of the Majority should always prevail. If they approve the proposed Convention in all it's parts, I shall concur in it chearfully, in hopes that they will amend it whenever they shall find it work wrong. I think our governments will remain virtuous for many centuries; as long as they are chiefly agricultural; and this will be as long as there shall be vacant lands in any part of America. When they get piled upon one another in large cities, as in Europe, they will become corrupt as in Europe. Above all things I hope the education of the common people will be attended to; convinced that on their good sense we may rely with the most security for the preservation of a due degree of liberty. I have tired you by this time with my disquisitions and will therefore only add assurances of the sincerity of those sentiments of esteem and attachment with which I am Dear Sir your affectionate friend & servant,   TH: JEFFERSON

P.S. The instability of our laws is really an immense evil. I think it would be well to provide in our constitutions that there shall always be a twelvemonth between the ingrossing a bill and passing it: that it should then be offered to it's passage without changing a word: and that if circumstances should be thought to require a speedier passage, it should take two thirds of both houses instead of a bare majority.

TO FRANCIS HOPKINSON *

DEAR SIR   Paris Mar. 13. 1789.

Since my last, which was of Dec. 21. yours of Dec. 9. and 21. are received. Accept my thanks for the papers and pamphlets which accompanied them, and mine and my daughter's for the book of songs. I will not tell you how much they have pleased us nor how well the last of them merits praise for it's pathos, but relate a fact only, which is that while my elder daughter was playing it on the harpsichord, I happened to look towards the fire and saw the younger one all in tears. I asked her if she was sick? She said "no; but the tune was so mournful."— The Editor of the Encyclopedie has published something as to an advanced price on his future volumes, which I understand alarms the subscribers. It was in a paper which I do not take and therefore I have not yet seen it, nor can say what it is.—I hope that by this time you have ceased to make wry faces about your vinegar, and that

* Boyd, 14:649–51.

you have received it safe and good. You say that I have
been dished up to you as an antifederalist, and ask me
if it be just. My opinion was never worthy enough of
notice to merit citing: but since you ask it I will tell it
you. I am not a Federalist, because I never submitted the
whole system of my opinions to the creed of any party
of men whatever in religion, in philosophy, in politics,
or in any thing else where I was capable of thinking for
myself. Such an addiction is the last degradation of a
free and moral agent. If I could not go to heaven but
with a party, I would not go there at all. Therefore I
protest to you I am not of the party of federalists. But I
am much farther from that of the Antifederalists. I approved from the first moment, of the great mass of what
is in the new constitution, the consolidation of the government, the organisation into Executive, legislative and
judiciary, the subdivision of the legislative, the happy
compromise of interests between the great and little
states by the different manner of voting in the different
houses, the voting by persons instead of states, the qualified negative on laws given to the Executive which however I should have liked better if associated with the
judiciary also as in New York, and the power of taxation.
I thought at first that the latter might have been limited.
A little reflection soon convinced me it ought not to be.
What I disapproved from the first moment also was the
want of a bill of rights to guard liberty against the legislative as well as executive branches of the government,
that is to say to secure freedom in religion, freedom of
the press, freedom from monopolies, freedom from unlawful imprisonment, freedom from a permanent military, and a trial by jury in all cases determinable by the
laws of the land. I disapproved also the perpetual re-
eligibility of the President. To these points of disapprobation I adhere. My first wish was that the 9. first
conventions might accept the constitution, as the means
of securing to us the great mass of good it contained, and
that the 4. last might reject it, as the means of obtaining
amendments. But I was corrected in this wish the moment I saw the much better plan of Massachusets and

which had never occurred to me. With respect to the declaration of rights I suppose the majority of the United states are of my opinion: for I apprehend all the antifederalists, and a very respectable proportion of the federalists think that such a declaration should now be annexed. The enlightened part of Europe have given us the greatest credit for inventing this instrument of security for the rights of the people, and have been not a little surprised to see us so soon give it up. With respect to the re-eligibility of the president, I find myself differing from the majority of my countrymen, for I think there are but three states of the 11. which have desired an alteration of this. And indeed, since the thing is established, I would wish it not to be altered during the life of our great leader, whose executive talents are superior to those I beleive of any man in the world, and who alone by the authority of his name and the confidence reposed in his perfect integrity, is fully qualified to put the new government so under way as to secure it against the efforts of opposition. But having derived from our error all the good there was in it I hope we shall correct it the moment we can no longer have the same person at the helm. These, my dear friend, are my sentiments, by which you will see I was right in saying I am neither federalist nor antifederalist; that I am of neither party, nor yet a trimmer between parties. These my opinions I wrote within a few hours after I had read the constitution, to one or two friends in America. I had not then read one single word printed on the subject. I never had an opinion in politics or religion which I was afraid to own. A costive reserve on these subjects might have procured me more esteem from some people, but less from myself. My great wish is to go on in a strict but silent performance of my duty: to avoid attracting notice and to keep my name out of newspapers, because I find the pain of a little censure, even when it is unfounded, is more acute than the pleasure of much praise. The attaching circumstance of my present office is that I can do it's duties unseen by those for whom they are done.— You did not think, by so short a phrase in your letter, to have drawn on yourself such an egoistical dissertation. I beg your pardon for it, and will endeavor to merit that pardon by the constant sentiments of esteem & attachment with which I am Dear Sir, Your sincere friend & servant,   TH: JEFFERSON

P.S. Affectionate respects to Dr. Franklin Mr. Rittenhouse, their and your good families.

TO JAMES MADISON *

Monticello, November 17, 1798.

Mr. Richardson has been detained by several jobs indespensible to the progress of the carpenters, & to the securing what is done against winter. When will Whitten be done with you? or could you by any means dispense with his services till I set out for Philadelphia? My floors can only be laid while I am at home, and I can not get a workman here. Perhaps you have some other with you or near you who could go on with your work till his return to you. I only mention these things that if you have any other person who could enable you to spare him a few weeks, I could employ him to much accommodation till my departure in laying my floors. But in this consult your own convenience only.

I enclose you a copy of the draught of the Kentucky resolves. I think we should distinctly affirm all the important principles they contain, so as to hold to that ground in future, and leave the matter in such a train as that we may not be committed absolutely to push the matter to extremities, & yet may be free to push as far as events will render prudent. I think to set out so as to arrive in Philadelphia the Saturday before Christmas. My friendly respects to mrs. Madison, to your father & family; health, happiness & adieu to yourself.

40. lbs. of [ ] nails @ 14½d per lb. were sent this

* Paul L. Ford, ed., *The Writings of Thomas Jefferson* (New York: G. P. Putnam's Sons, 1892–1899), 7:288.

morning, being all we had. They contained (according to the count of a single pound) 314 × 40 = 12.560.

THE KENTUCKY RESOLUTIONS OF 1798*

FAIR COPY.

1. *Resolved,* That the several States composing the United States of America, are not united on the principle of unlimited submission to their general government; but that, by a compact under the style and title of a Constitution for the United States, and of amendments thereto, they constituted a general government for special purposes,—delegated to that government certain definite powers, reserving, each State to itself, the residuary mass of right to their own self-government; and that whensoever the general government assumes undelegated powers, its acts are unauthoritative, void, and of no force: that to this compact each State acceded as a State, and is an integral party, its co-States forming, as to itself, the other party: that the government created by this compact was not made the exclusive or final judge of the extent of the powers delegated to itself; since that would have made its discretion, and not the Constitution, the measure of its powers; but that, as in all other cases of compact among powers having no common judge, each party has an equal right to judge for itself, as well of infractions as of the mode and measure of redress.

2. *Resolved,* That the Constitution of the United States having delegated to Congress a power to punish treason, counterfeiting the securities and current coin of the United States, piracies, and felonies committed on the high seas, and offences against the law of nations, and no other crimes whatsoever; and it being true as a general principle, and one of the amendments to the Constitution having also declared, that "the powers not delegated to the United States by the Constitution, nor

* Ford, 7:289–308.

prohibited by it to the States, are reserved to the States respectively, or to the people," therefore the act of Congress, passed on the 14th day of July, 1798, and intituled "An Act in addition to the act intituled An Act for the punishment of certain crimes against the United States," as also the act passed by them on the — day of June, 1798, intituled "An Act to punish frauds committed on the bank of the United States," (and all their other acts which assume to create, define, or punish crimes, other than those so enumerated in the Constitution,) are altogether void, and of no force; and that the power to create, define, and punish such other crimes is reserved, and, of right, appertains solely and exclusively to the respective States, each within its own territory.

3. *Resolved,* That it is true as a general principle, and is also expressly declared by one of the amendments to the Constitution, that "the powers not delegated to the United States by the Constitution, nor prohibited by it to the States, are reserved to the States respectively, or to the people"; and that no power over the freedom of religion, freedom of speech, or freedom of the press being delegated to the United States by the Constitution, nor prohibited by it to the States, all lawful powers respecting the same did of right remain, and were reserved to the States or the people: that thus was manifested their determination to retain to themselves the right of judging how far the licentiousness of speech and of the press may be abridged without lessening their useful freedom, and how far those abuses which cannot be separated from their use should be tolerated, rather than the use be destroyed. And thus also they guarded against all abridgment by the United States of the freedom of religious opinions and exercises, and retained to themselves the right of protecting the same, as this State, by a law passed on the general demand of its citizens, had already protected them from all human restraint or interference. And that in addition to this general principle and express declaration, another and more special provision has been made by one of the amendments to the Constitution, which expressly declares, that "Con-

gress shall make no law respecting an establishment of religion, or prohibiting the free exercise thereof, or abridging the freedom of speech or of the press": thereby guarding in the same sentence, and under the same words, the freedom of religion, of speech, and of the press: insomuch, that whatever violates either, throws down the sanctuary which covers the others, and that libels, falsehood, and defamation, equally with heresy and false religion, are withheld from the cognizance of federal tribunals. That, therefore, the act of Congress of the United States, passed on the 14th day of July, 1798, intituled "An Act in addition to the act intituled An Act for the punishment of certain crimes against the United States," which does abridge the freedom of the press, is not law, but is altogether void, and of no force.

4. *Resolved,* That alien friends are under the jurisdiction and protection of the laws of the State wherein they are: that no power over them has been delegated to the United States, nor prohibited to the individual States, distinct from their power over citizens. And it being true as a general principle, and one of the amendments to the Constitution having also declared, that "the powers not delegated to the United States by the Constitution, nor prohibited by it to the States, are reserved to the States respectively, or to the people," the act of the Congress of the United States, passed on the — day of July, 1798, intituled "An Act concerning aliens," which assumes powers over alien friends, not delegated by the Constitution, is not law, but is altogether void, and of no force.

5. *Resolved,* That in addition to the general principle, as well as the express declaration, that powers not delegated are reserved, another and more special provision, inserted in the Constitution from abundant caution, has declared that "the migration or importation of such persons as any of the States now existing shall think proper to admit, shall not be prohibited by the Congress prior to the year 1808": that this commonwealth does admit the migration of alien friends, described as the subject of the said act concerning aliens: that a provision against

THE PRECIOUS BLESSING OF LIBERTY   45

prohibiting their migration, is a provision against all acts equivalent thereto, or it would be nugatory: that to remove them when migrated, is equivalent to a prohibition of their migration, and is, therefore, contrary to the said provision of the Constitution, and void.

6. *Resolved,* That the imprisonment of a person under the protection of the laws of this commonwealth, on his failure to obey the simple *order* of the President to depart out of the United States, as is undertaken by said act intituled "An Act concerning aliens," is contrary to the Constitution, one amendment to which has provided that "no person shall be deprived of liberty without due process of law"; and that another having provided that "in all criminal prosecutions the accused shall enjoy the right to public trial by an impartial jury, to be informed of the nature and cause of the accusation, to be confronted with the witnesses against him, to have compulsory process for obtaining witnesses in his favor, and to have the assistance of counsel for his defence," the same act, undertaking to authorize the President to remove a person out of the United States, who is under the protection of the law, on his own suspicion, without accusation, without jury, without public trial, without confrontation of the witnesses against him, without hearing witnesses in his favor, without defence, without counsel, is contrary to the provision also of the Constitution, is therefore not law, but utterly void, and of no force: that transferring the power of judging any person, who is under the protection of the laws, from the courts to the President of the United States, as is undertaken by the same act concerning aliens, is against the article of the Constitution which provides that "the judicial power of the United States shall be vested in courts, the judges of which shall hold their offices during good behavior"; and that the said act is void for that reason also. And it is further to be noted, that this transfer of judiciary power is to that magistrate of the general government who already possesses all the Executive, and a negative on all Legislative powers.

7. *Resolved,* That the construction applied by the

General Government (as is evidenced by sundry of their proceedings) to those parts of the Constitution of the United States which delegate to Congress a power "to lay and collect taxes, duties, imposts, and excises, to pay the debts, and provide for the common defence and general welfare of the United States," and "to make all laws which shall be necessary and proper for carrying into execution the powers vested by the Constitution in the government of the United States, or in any department or officer thereof," goes to the destruction of all limits prescribed to their power by the Constitution: that words meant by the instrument to be subsidiary only to the execution of limited powers, ought not to be so construed as themselves to give unlimited powers, nor a part to be so taken as to destroy the whole residue of that instrument: that the proceedings of the General Government under color of these articles, will be a fit and necessary subject of revisal and correction, at a time of greater tranquillity, while those specified in the preceding resolutions call for immediate redress.

8th. *Resolved,* That a committee of conference and correspondence be appointed, who shall have in charge to communicate the preceding resolutions to the Legislatures of the several States; to assure them that this commonwealth continues in the same esteem of their friendship and union which it has manifested from that moment at which a common danger first suggested a common union: that it considers union, for specified national purposes, and particularly to those specified in the late federal compact, to be friendly to the peace, happiness, the prosperity of all the States: that faithful to that compact, according to the plain intent and meaning in which it was understood and acceded to by the several parties, it is sincerely anxious for its preservation: that it does also believe, that to take from the States all the powers of self-government and transfer them to a general and consolidated government, without regard to the special delegations and reservations solemnly agreed to in that compact, is not for the peace, happiness, or prosperity of these States; and that therefore this commonwealth is determined, as it doubts not its co-States are, to submit to undelegated, and consequently unlimited powers in no man, or body of men on earth: that in cases of an abuse of the delegated powers, the members of the general government, being chosen by the people, a change by the people would be the constitutional remedy; but, where powers are assumed which have not been delegated, a nullification of the act is the rightful remedy: that every State has a natural right in cases not within the compact, (casus non fœderis,) to nullify of their own authority all assumptions of power by others within their limits: that without this right they would be under the dominion, absolute and unlimited, of whosoever might exercise this right of judgment for them: that nevertheless, this commonwealth, from motives of regard and respect for its co-States, has wished to communicate with them on the subject: that with them alone it is proper to communicate, they alone being parties to the compact, and solely authorized to judge in the last resort of the powers exercised under it, Congress being not a party, but merely the creature of the compact, and subject as to its assumptions of power to the final judgment of those by whom, and for whose use itself and its powers were all created and modified: that if the acts before specified should stand, these conclusions would flow from them; that the general government may place any act they think proper on the list of crimes, and punish it themselves whether enumerated or not enumerated by the constitution as cognizable by them: that they may transfer its cognizance to the President, or any other person, who may himself be the accuser, counsel, judge and jury, whose *suspicions* may be the evidence, his *order* the sentence, his *officer* the executioner, and his breast the sole record of the transaction: that a very numerous and valuable description of the inhabitants of these States being, by this precedent, reduced, as outlaws, to the absolute dominion of one man, and the barrier of the Constitution thus swept away from us all, no rampart now remains against the passions and the powers of a majority in Congress to protect from

a like exportation, or other more grievous punishment
the minority of the same body, the legislatures, judges,
governors and counsellors of the States, nor their other
peaceable inhabitants, who may venture to reclaim the
constitutional rights and liberties of the States and
people, or who for other causes, good or bad, may be
obnoxious to the views, or marked by the suspicions of
the President, or be thought dangerous to his or their
election, or other interests public or personal: that the
friendless alien has indeed been selected as the safest
subject of a first experiment; but the citizen will soon
follow, or rather, has already followed, for already has a
sedition act marked him as its prey: that these and successive acts of the same character, unless arrested at the
threshold, necessarily drive these States into revolution
and blood, and will furnish new calumnies against republican government, and new pretexts for those who
wish it to be believed that man cannot be governed but
by a rod of iron: that it would be a dangerous delusion
were a confidence in the men of our choice to silence our
fears for the safety of our rights: that confidence is everywhere the parent of despotism—free government is
founded in jealousy, and not in confidence; it is jealousy
and not confidence which prescribes limited constitutions, to bind down those whom we are obliged to trust
with power: that our Constitution has accordingly fixed
the limits to which, and no further, our confidence may
go; and let the honest advocate of confidence read the
Alien and Sedition acts, and say if the Constitution has
not been wise in fixing limits to the government it
created, and whether we should be wise in destroying
those limits. Let him say what the government is, if it be
not a tyranny, which the men of our choice have conferred on our President, and the President of our choice
has assented to, and accepted over the friendly strangers
to whom the mild spirit of our country and its laws have
pledged hospitality and protection: that the men of our
choice have more respected the bare *suspicions* of the
President, than the solid right of innocence, the claims
of justification, the sacred force of truth and the forms

and substance of law and justice. In questions of power, then, let no more be heard of confidence in man, but bind him down from mischief by the chains of the Constitution. That this commonwealth does therefore call on its co-States for an expression of their sentiments on the acts concerning aliens, and for the punishment of certain crimes herein before specified, plainly declaring whether these acts are or are not authorized by the federal compact. And it doubts not that their sense will be so announced as to prove their attachment unaltered to limited government, whether general or particular. And that the rights and liberties of their co-States will be exposed to no dangers by remaining embarked in a common bottom with their own. That they will concur with this commonwealth in considering the said acts as so palpably against the Constitution as to amount to an undisguised declaration that that compact is not meant to be the measure of the powers of the General Government, but that it will proceed in the exercise over these States, of all powers whatsoever: that they will view this as seizing the rights of the States, and consolidating them in the hands of the General Government, with a power assumed to bind the States, (not merely in the cases made federal, (casus fœderis), but) in all cases whatsoever, by laws made, not with their consent, but by others against their consent; that this would be to surrender the form of government we have chosen, and live under one deriving its powers from its own will, and not from our authority; and that the co-States, recurring to their natural right in cases not made federal, will concur in declaring these acts void, and of no force, and will each take measures of its own for providing that neither these acts, nor any others of the General Government not plainly and intentionally authorized by the Constitution, shall be exercised within their respective territories.

9th. *Resolved,* That the said committee be authorized to communicate by writing or personal conferences, at any times or places whatever, with any person or persons who may be appointed by any one or more co-States to

correspond or confer with them; and that they lay their
proceedings before the next session of Assembly.

FIRST INAUGURAL ADDRESS*

AT WASHINGTON, D. C., MARCH 4, 1801.

Friends and Fellow-Citizens:

Called upon to undertake the duties of the first executive office of our country, I avail myself of the presence
of that portion of my fellow-citizens which is here assembled to express my grateful thanks for the favor with
which they have been pleased to look toward me, to declare a sincere consciousness that the task is above my
talents, and that I approach it with those anxious and
awful presentiments which the greatness of the charge
and the weakness of my powers so justly inspire. A rising
nation, spread over a wide and fruitful land, traversing
all the seas with the rich productions of their industry,
engaged in commerce with nations who feel power and
forget right, advancing rapidly to destinies beyond the
reach of mortal eye—when I contemplate these tran-
scendent objects, and see the honor, the happiness, and
the hopes of this beloved country committed to the issue
and the auspices of this day, I shrink from the contemplation, and humble myself before the magnitude of the
undertaking. Utterly, indeed, should I despair did not
the presence of many whom I here see remind me that
in the other high authorities provided by our Constitution I shall find resources of wisdom, of virtue, and of
zeal on which to rely under all difficulties. To you, then,
gentlemen, who are charged with the sovereign functions
of legislation, and to those associated with you, I look
with encouragement for that guidance and support
which may enable us to steer with safety the vessel in

* James D. Richardson, *A Compilation of the Messages and Papers
of the Presidents, 1797–1897* (Washington, D. C.: Government Printing Office, 1896), 1:321–24.

which we are all embarked amidst the conflicting elements of a troubled world.

During the contest of opinion through which we have passed the animation of discussions and of exertions has sometimes worn an aspect which might impose on strangers unused to think freely and to speak and to write what they think; but this being now decided by the voice of the nation, announced according to the rules of the Constitution, all will, of course, arrange themselves under the will of the law, and unite in common efforts for the common good. All, too, will bear in mind this sacred principle, that though the will of the majority is in all cases to prevail, that will to be rightful must be reasonable; that the minority possess their equal rights, which equal law must protect, and to violate would be oppression. Let us, then, fellow-citizens, unite with one heart and one mind. Let us restore to social intercourse that harmony and affection without which liberty and even life itself are but dreary things. And let us reflect that, having banished from our land that religious intolerance under which mankind so long bled and suffered, we have yet gained little if we countenance a political intolerance as despotic, as wicked, and capable of as bitter and bloody persecutions. During the throes and convulsions of the ancient world, during the agonizing spasms of infuriated man, seeking through blood and slaughter his long-lost liberty, it was not wonderful that the agitation of the billows should reach even this distant and peaceful shore; that this should be more felt and feared by some and less by others, and should divide opinions as to measures of safety. But every difference of opinion is not a difference of principle. We have called by different names brethren of the same principle. We are all Republicans, we are all Federalists. If there be any among us who would wish to dissolve this Union or to change its republican form, let them stand undisturbed as monuments of the safety with which error of opinion may be tolerated where reason is left free to combat it. I know, indeed, that some honest men fear that a republican government can not be strong, that this Government is not strong enough; but would the honest patriot, in the full tide of successful experiment, abandon a government which has so far kept us free and firm on the theoretic and visionary fear that this Government, the world's best hope, may by possibility want energy to preserve itself? I trust not. I believe this, on the contrary, the strongest Government on earth. I believe it the only one where every man, at the call of the law, would fly to the standard of the law, and would meet invasions of the public order as his own personal concern. Sometimes it is said that man can not be trusted with the government of himself. Can he, then, be trusted with the government of others? Or have we found angels in the forms of kings to govern him? Let history answer this question.

Let us, then, with courage and confidence pursue our own Federal and Republican principles, our attachment to union and representative government. Kindly separated by nature and a wide ocean from the exterminating havoc of one quarter of the globe; too high-minded to endure the degradations of the others; possessing a chosen country, with room enough for our descendants to the thousandth and thousandth generation; entertaining a due sense of our equal right to the use of our own faculties, to the acquisitions of our own industry, to honor and confidence from our fellow-citizens, resulting not from birth, but from our actions and their sense of them; enlightened by a benign religion, professed, indeed, and practiced in various forms, yet all of them inculcating honesty, truth, temperance, gratitude, and the love of man; acknowledging and adoring an overruling Providence, which by all its dispensations proves that it delights in the happiness of man here and his greater happiness hereafter—with all these blessings, what more is necessary to make us a happy and a prosperous people? Still one thing more, fellow-citizens—a wise and frugal Government, which shall restrain men from injuring one another, shall leave them otherwise free to regulate their own pursuits of industry and improvement, and shall not take from the mouth of labor the bread it has earned. This is the sum of good government, and this is necessary to close the circle of our felicities.

About to enter, fellow-citizens, on the exercise of duties which comprehend everything dear and valuable to you, it is proper you should understand what I deem the essential principles of our Government, and consequently those which ought to shape its Administration. I will compress them within the narrowest compass they will bear, stating the general principle, but not all its limitations. Equal and exact justice to all men, of whatever state or persuasion, religious or political; peace, commerce, and honest friendship with all nations, entangling alliances with none; the support of the State governments in all their rights, as the most competent administrations for our domestic concerns and the surest bulwarks against antirepublican tendencies; the preservation of the General Government in its whole constitutional vigor, as the sheet anchor of our peace at home and safety abroad; a jealous care of the right of election by the people—a mild and safe corrective of abuses which are lopped by the sword of revolution where peaceable remedies are unprovided; absolute acquiescence in the decisions of the majority, the vital principle of republics, from which is no appeal but to force, the vital principle and immediate parent of despotism; a well-disciplined militia, our best reliance in peace and for the first moments of war, till regulars may relieve them; the supremacy of the civil over the military authority; economy in the public expense, that labor may be lightly burthened; the honest payment of our debts and sacred preservation of the public faith; encouragement of agriculture, and of commerce as its handmaid; the diffusion of information and arraignment of all abuses at the bar of the public reason; freedom of religion; freedom of the press, and freedom of person under the protection of the habeas corpus, and trial by juries impartially selected. These principles form the bright constellation which has gone before us and guided our steps through an age of revolution and reformation. The wisdom of our sages and blood of our heroes have been devoted to their attainment. They should be the creed of our political faith, the text of civic instruction, the touchstone by which to try the services of those we trust; and should we wander from them in moments of error or of alarm, let us hasten to retrace our steps and to regain the road which alone leads to peace, liberty, and safety.

I repair, then, fellow-citizens, to the post you have assigned me. With experience enough in subordinate offices to have seen the difficulties of this the greatest of all, I have learnt to expect that it will rarely fall to the lot of imperfect man to retire from this station with the reputation and the favor which bring him into it. Without pretensions to that high confidence you reposed in our first and greatest revolutionary character, whose preeminent services had entitled him to the first place in his country's love and destined for him the fairest page in the volume of faithful history, I ask so much confidence only as may give firmness and effect to the legal administration of your affairs. I shall often go wrong through defect of judgment. When right, I shall often be thought wrong by those whose positions will not command a view of the whole ground. I ask your indulgence for my own errors, which will never be intentional, and your support against the errors of others, who may condemn what they would not if seen in all its parts. The approbation implied by your suffrage is a great consolation to me for the past, and my future solicitude will be to retain the good opinion of those who have bestowed it in advance, to conciliate that of others by doing them all the good in my power, and to be instrumental to the happiness and freedom of all.

Relying, then, on the patronage of your good will, I advance with obedience to the work, ready to retire from it whenever you become sensible how much better choice it is in your power to make. And may that Infinite Power which rules the destinies of the universe lead our councils to what is best, and give them a favorable issue for your peace and prosperity.

TO THOMAS SEYMOUR*

Washington, February 11, 1807.

SIR,—The mass of business which occurs during a session of the Legislature, renders me necessarily unpunctual in acknowledging the receipt of letters, and in answering those which will admit of delay. This must be my apology for being so late in noticing the receipt of the letter of December 20th, addressed to me by yourself, and several other republican characters of your State of high respectability. I have seen with deep concern the afflicting oppression under which the republican citizens of Connecticut suffer from an unjust majority. The truths expressed in your letter have been long exposed to the nation through the channel of the public papers, and are the more readily believed because most of the States during the momentary ascendancy of kindred majorities in them, have seen the same spirit of oppression prevail.

With respect to the countervailing prosecutions now instituted in the Court of the U S in Connecticut, I had heard but little, & certainly, I believe, never expressed a sentiment on them. That a spirit of indignation and retaliation should arise when an opportunity should present itself, was too much within the human constitution to excite either surprise or censure, and confined to an appeal to truth only, it cannot lessen the useful freedom of the press.

As to myself, conscious that there was not a *truth* on earth which I feared should be known, I have lent myself willingly as the subject of a great experiment, which was to prove that an administration, conducting itself with integrity and common understanding, cannot be battered down, even by the falsehoods of a licentious press, and consequently still less by the press, as restrained within the legal & wholesome limits of truth. This experiment was wanting for the world to demon-

* Ford, 9:28–31.

strate the falsehood of the pretext that freedom of the press is incompatible with orderly government. I have never therefore even contradicted the thousands of calumnies so industriously propagated against myself. But the fact being once established, that the press is impotent when it abandons itself to falsehood, I leave to others to restore it to it's strength, by recalling it within the pale of truth. Within that it is a noble institution, equally the friend of science & of civil liberty. If this can once be effected in your State, I trust we shall soon see it's citizens rally to the republican principles of our Constitution, which unite their sister-States into one family. It would seem impossible that an intelligent people, with the faculty of reading & right of thinking, should continue much longer to slumber under the pupilage of an interested aristocracy of priests & lawyers, persuading them to distrust themselves, & to let them think for them. I sincerely wish that your efforts may awaken them from this voluntary degradation of mind, restore them to a due estimate of themselves & their fellow-citizens, and a just abhorrence of the falsehoods & artifices which have seduced them. Experience of the use made by federalism of whatever comes from me, obliges me to suggest the caution of considering my letter as private. I pray you to present me respectfully to the other gentlemen who joined in the letter to me, & to whom this is equally addressed, and to accept yourself my salutations, & assurances of great esteem & consideration.

TO MONSIEUR N. G. DUFIEF*

Monticello, April 19, 1814.

DEAR SIR,—Your favor of the 6th instant is just received, and I shall with equal willingness and truth, state the degree of agency you had, respecting the copy of M. de Becourt's book, which came to my hands. That

* Andrew A. Lipscomb and A. E. Bergh, eds., *The Writings of Thomas Jefferson* (Washington, D. C.: Thomas Jefferson Memorial Association, 1903), 14:126–29.

gentleman informed me, by letter, that he was about to publish a volume in French, "Sur la Création du Monde, un Système d'Organisation Primitive," which, its title promised to be, either a geological or astronomical work. I subscribed; and, when published, he sent me a copy; and as you were my correspondent in the book line in Philadelphia, I took the liberty of desiring him to call on you for the price, which, he afterwards informed me, you were so kind as to pay him for me, being, I believe, two dollars. But the sole copy which came to me was from himself directly, and, as far as I know, was never seen by you.

I am really mortified to be told that, *in the United States of America,* a fact like this can become a subject of inquiry, and of criminal inquiry too, as an offence against religion; that a question about the sale of a book can be carried before the civil magistrate. Is this then our freedom of religion? and are we to have a censor whose imprimatur shall say what books may be sold, and what we may buy? And who is thus to dogmatize religious opinions for our citizens? Whose foot is to be the measure to which ours are all to be cut or stretched? Is a priest to be our inquisitor, or shall a layman, simple as ourselves, set up his reason as the rule for what we are to read, and what we must believe? It is an insult to our citizens to question whether they are rational beings or not, and blasphemy against religion to suppose it cannot stand the test of truth and reason. If M. de Becourt's book be false in its facts, disprove them; if false in its reasoning, refute it. But, for God's sake, let us freely hear both sides, if we choose. I know little of its contents, having barely glanced over here and there a passage, and over the table of contents. From this, the Newtonian philosophy seemed the chief object of attack, the issue of which might be trusted to the strength of the two combatants; Newton certainly not needing the auxiliary arm of the government, and still less the holy Author of our religion, as to what in it concerns Him. I thought the work would be very innocent, and one which might be confided to the reason of any man; not likely to be much read if let alone, but, if persecuted, it will be generally read. Every man in the United States will think it a duty to buy a copy, in vindication of his right to buy, and to read what he pleases. I have just been reading the new constitution of Spain. One of its fundamental bases is expressed in these words: "The *Roman Catholic* religion, the only true one, is, and always shall be, that of the Spanish nation. The government protects it by wise and just laws, and prohibits the exercise of any other whatever." Now I wish this presented to those who question what you may sell, or we may buy, with a request to strike out the words, "Roman Catholic," and to insert the denomination of their own religion. This would ascertain the code of dogmas which each wishes should domineer over the opinions of all others, and be taken, like the Spanish religion, under the "protection of wise and just laws." It would show to what they wish to reduce the liberty for which one generation has sacrificed life and happiness. It would present our boasted freedom of religion as a thing of theory only, and not of practice, as what would be a poor exchange for the theoretic thraldom, but practical freedom of Europe. But it is impossible that the laws of Pennsylvania, which set us the first example of the wholesome and happy effects of religious freedom, can permit the inquisitorial functions to be proposed to their courts. Under them you are surely safe.

At the date of yours of the 6th, you had not received mine of the 3d instant, asking a copy of an edition of Newton's Principia, which I had seen advertised. When the cost of that shall be known, it shall be added to the balance of $4.93, and incorporated with a larger remittance I have to make to Philadelphia. Accept the assurance of my great esteem and respect.

2: The Free Exercise of Religion

"Our particular principles of religion are a
subject of accountability to our God alone."

*The letter to Dufief which closed the preceding section
forcefully demonstrates how, for Jefferson, one of the
greatest threats to the free mind was dogmatic religion.
The liberty Jefferson championed was at bottom the
freedom to believe and he found the most critical restrictions on that freedom to be traceable to the policies
and practices of one or another church, especially as
churches and states maintained alliances. John Locke
had said that "no man can, if he would, conform his
faith to the dictates of another. All the life and power
of . . . true and saving religion consists in the inward
persuasion of the mind, without which nothing can be
acceptable to God." Jefferson, insisting that religion
cannot be extended except by means of "influence on
reason alone," carried the Lockean doctrine farther,
making it central to his entire intellectual framework.
To advance such an orientation required the elimina-
tion of the traditional interrelationships of church and
state.*

*As in the political, so in the educational sphere,
Jefferson was pledged to disestablishment of religion.
In the* Notes on the State of Virginia, *written in response to the queries of the French diplomat and
encyclopedist, Marbois, Jefferson took the opportunity
to spell out the problem of religious freedom as he
saw it in Virginia and to set forth the logic for divorcing
the civil from the ecclesiastical in public affairs. This
approach was climaxed in the adoption by the Virginia*

Assembly of the famous Statute of Religious Freedom, a statement which Jefferson regarded as one of the crowning achievements of his career and which stands as the epitome of the theory of church-state separation in a democracy. The application of this doctrine to government, to the pulpit, and especially to the school is detailed in Jefferson's famous response to the Danbury Baptist Association and the letters to Samuel Miller, P. H. Wendover, and Thomas Cooper which follow. Perhaps Jefferson's most elaborate discussion of his understanding of the practical meaning of the separation principle, as well as further illumination of his own religious attitudes, is to be found in the Annual Report of the Board of Visitors of the University of Virginia dated October 7, 1822, from which an excerpt is here reprinted.

SEE ALSO:

"Notes and Proceedings on Discontinuing the Establishment of the Church of England" [11 October to 9 December 1776] (Boyd, 1:525–58, especially 544–50).
Letter to John Adams, August 22, 1813 (Ford, 9:408–19).
Letter to Miles King, September 26, 1814 (Washington, 6:388).
Letter to Charles Thomson, January 29, 1817 (Ford, 10:242–44).

NOTES ON THE STATE OF VIRGINIA*

QUERY XVII.

The different religions received into that state?

The first settlers in this country were emigrants from England, of the English church, just at a point of time

* Paul L. Ford, ed., *The Writings of Thomas Jefferson* (New York: G. P. Putnam's Sons, 1892–1899), 3:261–66.

when it was flushed with complete victory over the religious of all other persuasions. Possessed, as they became, of the powers of making, administering and executing the laws, they shewed equal intolerance in this country with their Presbyterian brethren, who had emigrated to the northern government. The poor Quakers were flying from persecution in England. They cast their eyes on these new countries as asylums of civil and religious freedom; but they found them free only for the reigning sect. Several acts of the Virginia assembly of 1659, 1662, and 1693, had made it penal in parents to refuse to have their children baptized; had prohibited the unlawful assembling of Quakers; had made it penal for any master of a vessel to bring a Quaker into the state; had ordered those already here, and such as should come thereafter, to be imprisoned till they should abjure the country; provided a milder punishment for their first and second return, but death for their third; had inhibited all persons from suffering their meetings in or near their houses, entertaining them individually, or disposing of books which supported their tenets. If no capital execution took place here, as did in New-England, it was not owing to the moderation of the church, or spirit of the legislature, as may be inferred from the law itself; but to historical circumstances which have not been handed down to us. The Anglicans retained full possession of the country about a century. Other opinions began then to creep in, and the great care of the government to support their own church, having begotten an equal degree of indolence in its clergy, two thirds of the people had become dissenters at the commencement of the present revolution. The laws indeed were still oppressive on them, but the spirit of one party had subsided into moderation, and of the other had risen to a degree of determination which commanded respect.

The present state of our laws on the subject of religion is this. The convention of May 1776, in their declaration of rights, declared it to be a truth, and a natural right, that the exercise of religion should be free; but when they proceeded to form on that declaration the ordinance of government, instead of taking up every principle declared in the bill of rights, and guarding it by legislative sanction, they passed over that which asserted our religious rights, leaving them as they found them. The same convention, however, when they met as a member of the general assembly in October 1776, repealed all *acts of parliament* which had rendered criminal the maintaining any opinions in matters of religion, the forbearing to repair to church, and the exercising any mode of worship; and suspended the laws giving salaries to the clergy, which suspension was made perpetual in October 1779. Statutory oppressions in religion being thus wiped away, we remain at present under those only imposed by the common law, or by our own acts of assembly. At the common law, *heresy* was a capital offence, punishable by burning. Its definition was left to the ecclesiastical judges, before whom the conviction was, till the statute of the 1 El. c. 1. circumscribed it, by declaring that nothing should be deemed heresy but what had been so determined by authority of the canonical scriptures, or by one of the four first general councils, or by some other council having for the grounds of their declaration the express and plain words of the scriptures. Heresy, thus circumscribed, being an offence at the common law, our act of assembly of October 1777, c. 17 gives cognizance of it to the general court, by declaring that the jurisdiction of that court shall be general in all matters at the common law. The execution is by the writ *De hæretico comburendo*. By our own act of assembly of 1705, c. 30, if a person brought up in the christian religion denies the being of a God, or the trinity, or asserts there are more Gods than one, or denies the christian religion to be true, or the scriptures to be of divine authority, he is punishable on the first offence by incapacity to hold any office or employment ecclesiastical, civil, or military; on the second by disability to sue, to take any gift or legacy, to be guardian, executor or administrator, and by three years imprisonment, without bail. A father's right to the custody of his own children being founded in law on his right of guardianship, this being taken away, they may of course be severed from him and put, by the authority of a court, into more orthodox hands. This is a summary view of that religious slavery under which a people have been willing to remain who have lavished their lives and fortunes for the establishment of their civil freedom. The error seems not sufficiently eradicated, that the operations of the mind, as well as the acts of the body, are subject to the coercion of the laws. But our rulers can have authority over such natural rights, only as we have submitted to them. The rights of conscience we never submitted, we could not submit. We are answerable for them to our God. The legitimate powers of government extend to such acts only as are injurious to others. But it does me no injury for my neighbor to say there are twenty gods, or no god. It neither picks my pocket nor breaks my leg. If it be said his testimony in a court of justice cannot be relied on, reject it then, and be the stigma on him. Constraint may make him worse by making him a hypocrite, but it will never make him a truer man. It may fix him obstinately in his errors, but will not cure them. Reason and free inquiry are the only effectual agents against error. Give a loose to them, they will support the true religion by bringing every false one to their tribunal, to the test of their investigation. They are the natural enemies of error, and of error only. Had not the Roman government permitted free inquiry, christianity could never have been introduced. Had not free inquiry been indulged, at the æra of the reformation, the corruptions of christianity could not have been purged away. If it be restrained now, the present corruptions will be protected, and new ones encouraged. Was the government to prescribe to us our medicine and diet, our bodies would be in such keeping as our souls are now. Thus in France the

emetic was once forbidden as a medicine, and the po-
tatoe as an article of food. Government is just as infallible, too, when it fixes systems in physics. Galileo
was sent to the inquisition for affirming that the earth
was a sphere; the government had declared it to be as
flat as a trencher, and Galileo was obliged to abjure
his error. This error however at length prevailed, the
earth became a globe, and Descartes declared it was
whirled round its axis by a vortex. The government
in which he lived was wise enough to see that this was
no question of civil jurisdiction, or we should all have
been involved by authority in vortices. In fact the
vortices have been exploded, and the Newtonian principle of gravitation is now more firmly established, on
the basis of reason, than it would be were the government to step in and to make it an article of necessary
faith. Reason and experiment have been indulged, and
error has fled before them. It is error alone which needs
the support of government. Truth can stand by itself.
Subject opinion to coercion: whom will you make your
inquisitors? Fallible men; men governed by bad passions,
by private as well as public reasons. And why subject
it to coercion? To produce uniformity. But is uniformity
of opinion desireable? No more than of face and stature.
Introduce the bed of Procrustes then, and as there is
danger that the large men may beat the small, make
us all of a size, by lopping the former and stretching
the latter. Difference of opinion is advantageous in
religion. The several sects perform the office of a Censor
morum over each other. Is uniformity attainable? Millions of innocent men, women and children, since the
introduction of Christianity, have been burnt, tortured,
fined, imprisoned: yet we have not advanced one inch
towards uniformity. What has been the effect of coercion? To make one half the world fools, and the other
half hypocrites. To support roguery and error all over
the earth. Let us reflect that it is inhabited by a thousand
millions of people. That these profess probably a
thousand different systems of religion. That ours is

but one of that thousand. That if there be but one right, and ours that one, we should wish to see the 999 wandering sects gathered into the fold of truth. But against such a majority we cannot effect this by force. Reason and persuasion are the only practicable instruments. To make way for these, free inquiry must be indulged; and how can we wish others to indulge it while we refuse it ourselves. But every state, says an inquisitor, has established some religion. "No two, say I, have established the same." Is this a proof of the infallibility of establishments? Our sister states of Pennsylvania and New York, however, have long subsisted without any establishment at all. The experiment was new and doubtful when they made it. It has answered beyond conception. They flourish infinitely. Religion is well supported; of various kinds indeed, but all good enough; all sufficient to preserve peace and order: or if a sect arises whose tenets would subvert morals, good sense has fair play, and reasons and laughs it out of doors, without suffering the state to be troubled with it. They do not hang more malefactors than we do. They are not more disturbed with religious dissentions. On the contrary, their harmony is unparalleled, and can be ascribed to nothing but their unbounded tolerance, because there is no other circumstance in which they differ from every nation on earth. They have made the happy discovery, that the way to silence religious disputes, is to take no notice of them. Let us too give this experiment fair play, and get rid, while we may, of those tyrannical laws. It is true we are as yet secured against them by the spirit of the times. I doubt whether the people of this country would suffer an execution for heresy, or a three years imprisonment for not comprehending the mysteries of the trinity. But is the spirit of the people an infallible, a permanent reliance? Is it government? Is this the kind of protection we receive in return for the rights we give up? Besides, the spirit of the times may alter, will alter. Our rulers will become corrupt, our people careless. A single zealot may commence persecuter, and better men be his victims. It can never be too often repeated, that the time for fixing every essential right on a legal basis is while our rulers are honest, and ourselves united. From the conclusion of this war we shall be going down hill. It will not then be necessary to resort every moment to the people for support. They will be forgotten therefore, and their rights disregarded. They will forget themselves, but in the sole faculty of making money, and will never think of uniting to effect a due respect for their rights. The shackles, therefore, which shall not be knocked off at the conclusion of this war, will remain on us long, will be made heavier and heavier, till our rights shall revive or expire in a convulsion.

A BILL FOR ESTABLISHING RELIGIOUS FREEDOM*

[This version is that of the Report of the Revisors, as introduced into the Virginia Assembly in 1779. The Bill was passed, with certain minor changes, in 1786.]

Well aware that the opinions and belief of men depend not on their own will, but follow involuntarily the evidence proposed to their minds; that Almighty God hath created the mind free, and manifested his supreme will that free it shall remain by making it altogether insusceptible of restraint; that all attempts to influence it by temporal punishments, or burthens, or by civil incapacitations, tend only to beget habits of hypocrisy and meanness, and are a departure from the plan of the holy author of our religion, who being lord both of body and mind, yet chose not to propagate it by coercions on either, as was in his Almighty power to do, but to extend it by its influence on reason alone; that the

* Julian P. Boyd, ed., *The Papers of Thomas Jefferson* (Princeton, N. J.: Princeton University Press, 1950 *et seq.*), 2:545-47.

impious presumption of legislators and rulers, civil as well as ecclesiastical, who, being themselves but fallible and uninspired men, have assumed dominion over the faith of others, setting up their own opinions and modes of thinking as the only true and infallible, and as such endeavoring to impose them on others, hath established and maintained false religions over the greatest part of the world and through all time: That to compel a man to furnish contributions of money for the propagation of opinions which he disbelieves and abhors, is sinful and tyrannical; that even the forcing him to support this or that teacher of his own religious persuasion, is depriving him of the comfortable liberty of giving his contributions to the particular pastor whose morals he would make his pattern, and whose powers he feels most persuasive to righteousness; and is withdrawing from the ministry those temporary rewards, which proceeding from an approbation of their personal conduct, are an additional incitement to earnest and unremitting labours for the instruction of mankind; that our civil rights have no dependance on our religious opinions, any more than our opinions in physics or geometry; that therefore the proscribing any citizen as unworthy the public confidence by laying upon him an incapacity of being called to offices of trust and emolument, unless he profess or renounce this or that religious opinion, is depriving him injuriously of those privileges and advantages to which, in common with his fellow citizens, he has a natural right; that it tends also to corrupt the principles of that very religion it is meant to encourage, by bribing, with a monopoly of worldly honours and emoluments, those who will externally profess and conform to it; that though indeed these are criminal who do not withstand such temptation, yet neither are those innocent who lay the bait in their way; that the opinions of men are not the object of civil government, nor under its jurisdiction; that to suffer the civil magistrate to intrude his powers into the field of opinion and to restrain the profession or propagation of principles on supposition of their ill tendency is a dangerous falacy, which at once destroys all religious liberty, because he being of course judge of that tendency will make his opinions the rule of judgment, and approve or condemn the sentiments of others only as they shall square with or differ from his own; that it is time enough for the rightful purposes of civil government for its officers to interfere when principles break out into overt acts against peace and good order; and finally, that truth is great and will prevail if left to herself; that she is the proper and sufficient antagonist to error, and has nothing to fear from the conflict unless by human interposition disarmed of her natural weapons, free argument and debate; errors ceasing to be dangerous when it is permitted freely to contradict them.

We the General Assembly of Virginia do enact that no man shall be compelled to frequent or support any religious worship, place, or ministry whatsoever, nor shall be enforced, restrained, molested, or burthened in his body or goods, nor shall otherwise suffer, on account of his religious opinions or belief; but that all men shall be free to profess, and by argument to maintain, their opinions in matters of religion, and that the same shall in no wise diminish, enlarge, or affect their civil capacities.

And though we well know that this Assembly, elected by the people for the ordinary purposes of legislation only, have no power to restrain the acts of succeeding Assemblies, constituted with powers equal to our own, and that therefore to declare this act irrevocable would be of no effect in law; yet we are free to declare, and do declare, that the rights hereby asserted are of the natural rights of mankind, and that if any act shall be hereafter passed to repeal the present or to narrow its operation, such act will be an infringement of natural right.

TO MESSRS. NEHEMIAH DODGE, EPHRAIM ROBBINS, AND STEPHEN S. NELSON, A COMMITTEE OF THE DANBURY BAPTIST ASSOCIATION, IN THE STATE OF CONNECTICUT*

Washington, January 1, 1802.

GENTLEMEN,—The affectionate sentiments of esteem and approbation which you are so good as to express towards me, on behalf of the Danbury Baptist Association, give me the highest satisfaction. My duties dictate a faithful and zealous pursuit of the interests of my constituents, and in proportion as they are persuaded of my fidelity to those duties, the discharge of them becomes more and more pleasing.

Believing with you that religion is a matter which lies solely between man and his God, that he owes account to none other for his faith or his worship, that the legislative powers of government reach actions only, and not opinions, I contemplate with sovereign reverence that act of the whole American people which declared that their legislature should "make no law respecting an establishment of religion, or prohibiting the free exercise thereof," thus building a wall of separation between Church and State. Adhering to this expression of the supreme will of the nation in behalf of the rights of conscience, I shall see with sincere satisfaction the progress of those sentiments which tend to restore to man all his natural rights, convinced he has no natural right in opposition to his social duties.

I reciprocate your kind prayers for the protection and blessing of the common Father and Creator of man, and tender you for yourselves and your religious association, assurances of my high respect and esteem.

* Andrew A. Lipscomb and A. E. Bergh, eds., *The Writings of Thomas Jefferson* (Washington, D. C.: Thomas Jefferson Memorial Association, 1903), 16:281–82.

TO REV. SAMUEL MILLER*

Washington, Jan. 23, 1808.

Sir,—I have duly received your favor of the 18th
and am thankful to you for having written it, because
it is more agreeable to prevent than to refuse what I
do not think myself authorized to comply with. I
consider the government of the US. as interdicted by
the Constitution from intermeddling with religious
institutions, their doctrines, discipline, or exercises.
This results not only from the provision that no law
shall be made respecting the establishment, or free
exercise, of religion, but from that also which reserves
to the states the powers not delegated to the U. S.
Certainly no power to prescribe any religious exercise,
or to assume authority in religious discipline, has been
delegated to the general government. It must then
rest with the states, as far as it can be in any human
authority. But it is only proposed that I should *recommend*, not prescribe a day of fasting & prayer. That is,
that I should *indirectly* assume to the U. S. an authority
over religious exercises which the Constitution has
directly precluded them from. It must be meant too that
this recommendation is to carry some authority, and
to be sanctioned by some penalty on those who dis-
regard it; not indeed of fine and imprisonment, but of
some degree of proscription perhaps in public opinion.
And does the change in the nature of the penalty make
the recommendation the less *a law* of conduct for
those to whom it is directed? I do not believe it is for
the interest of religion to invite the civil magistrate to
direct it's exercises, it's discipline, or it's doctrines;
nor of the religious societies that the general government should be invested with the power of effecting
any uniformity of time or matter among them. Fasting
& prayer are religious exercises. The enjoining them
an act of discipline. Every religious society has a right

* Ford, 9:174-76.

to determine for itself the times for these exercises, & the objects proper for them, according to their own particular tenets; and this right can never be safer than in their own hands, where the constitution has deposited it.

I am aware that the practice of my predecessors may be quoted. But I have ever believed that the example of state executives led to the assumption of that authority by the general government, without due examination, which would have discovered that what might be a right in a state government, was a violation of that right when assumed by another. Be this as it may, every one must act according to the dictates of his own reason, & mine tells me that civil powers alone have been given to the President of the US. and no authority to direct the religious exercises of his constituents.

I again express my satisfaction that you have been so good as to give me an opportunity of explaining myself in a private letter, in which I could give my reasons more in detail than might have been done in a public answer: and I pray you to accept the assurances of my high esteem & respect.

TO P. H. WENDOVER*

Monticello, March 13, 1815.

Sir,—Your favor of January the 30th was received after long delay on the road, and I have to thank you for the volume of discourses which you have been so kind as to send me. I have gone over them with great satisfaction, and concur with the able preacher in his estimate of the character of the belligerents in our late war, and lawfulness of defensive war. I consider the war, with him, as "made on good advice," that is, for just causes, and its dispensation as providential, inasmuch as it has exercised our patriotism and submission

* Lipscomb and Bergh, 14:279–84.

to order, has planted and invigorated among us arts of urgent necessity, has manifested the strong and the weak parts of our republican institutions, and the excellence of a representative democracy compared with the misrule of kings, has rallied the opinions of mankind to the natural rights of expatriation, and of a common property in the ocean, and raised us to that grade in the scale of nations which the bravery and liberality of our citizen soldiers, by land and by sea, the wisdom of our institutions and their observance of justice, entitled us to in the eyes of the world. All this Mr. McLeod has well proved, and from these sources of argument particularly which belong to his profession. On one question only I differ from him, and it is that which constitutes the subject of his first discourse, the right of discussing public affairs *in the pulpit*. I add the last words, because I admit the right in *general conversation* and in *writing;* in which last form it has been exercised in the valuable book you have now favored me with.

The mass of human concerns, moral and physical, is so vast, the field of knowledge requisite for man to conduct them to the best advantage is so extensive, that no human being can acquire the whole himself, and much less in that degree necessary for the instruction of others. It has of necessity, then, been distributed into different departments, each of which, singly, may give occupation enough to the whole time and attention of a single individual. Thus we have teachers of Languages, teachers of Mathematics, of Natural Philosophy, of Chemistry, of Medicine, of Law, of History, of Government, etc. Religion, too, is a separate department, and happens to be the only one deemed requisite for all men, however high or low. Collections of men associate together, under the name of congregations, and employ a religious teacher of the particular sect of opinions of which they happen to be, and contribute to make up a stipend as a compensation for the trouble of delivering them, at such periods as they agree on, lessons in the religion they profess. If they want instruction in other sciences or arts, they apply to other instructors; and this is generally the business of early life. But I suppose there is not an instance of a single congregation which has employed their preacher for the mixed purposes of lecturing them *from the pulpit* in Chemistry, in Medicine, in Law, in the science and principles of Government, or in anything but Religion exclusively. Whenever, therefore, preachers, instead of a lesson in religion, put them off with a discourse on the Copernican system, on chemical affinities, on the construction of government, or the characters or conduct of those administering it, it is a breach of contract, depriving their audience of the kind of service for which they are salaried, and giving them, instead of it, what they did not want, or, if wanted, would rather seek from better sources in that particular art or science. In choosing our pastor we look to his religious qualifications, without inquiring into his physical or political dogmas, with which we mean to have nothing to do. I am aware that arguments may be found, which may twist a thread of politics into the cord of religious duties. So may they for every other branch of human art or science. Thus, for example, it is a religious duty to obey the laws of our country; the teacher of religion, therefore, must instruct us in those laws, that we may know how to obey them. It is a religious duty to assist our sick neighbors; the preacher must, therefore, teach us medicine, that we may do it understandingly. It is a religious duty to preserve our own health; our religious teacher, then, must tell us what dishes are wholesome, and give us recipes in cookery, that we may learn how to prepare them. And so, ingenuity, by generalizing more and more, may amalgamate all the branches of science into any one of them, and the physician who is paid to visit the sick, may give a sermon instead of medicine, and the merchant to whom money is sent for a hat, may send a handkerchief instead of it. But notwithstanding this possible confusion of all sciences into one, common sense draws lines between them sufficiently distinct

for the general purposes of life, and no one is at a loss
to understand that a recipe in medicine or cookery,
or a demonstration in geometry, is not a lesson in
religion. I do not deny that a congregation may, if
they please, agree with their preacher that he shall
instruct them in Medicine also, or Law, or Politics.
Then, lectures in these, from the pulpit, become not
only a matter of right, but of duty also. But this must
be with the consent of every individual; because the
association being voluntary, the mere majority has no
right to apply the contributions of the minority to
purposes unspecified in the agreement of the congregation. I agree, too, that on all other occasions, the preacher
has the right, equally with every other citizen, to express his sentiments, in speaking or writing, on the
subjects of Medicine, Law, Politics, etc., his leisure
time being his own, and his congregation not obliged
to listen to his conversation or to read his writings;
and no one would have regretted more than myself,
had any scruple as to this right withheld from us the
valuable discourses which have led to the expression
of an opinion as to the true limits of the right. I feel
my portion of indebtment to the reverend author
for the distinguished learning, the logic and the eloquence with which he has proved that religion, as
well as reason, confirms the soundness of those principles on which our government has been founded and
its rights asserted.

These are my views on this question. They are in
opposition to those of the highly respected and able
preacher, and are, therefore, the more doubtingly offered.
Difference of opinion leads to inquiry, and inquiry
to truth; and that, I am sure, is the ultimate and
sincere object of us both. We both value too much the
freedom of opinion sanctioned by our Constitution, not
to cherish its exercise even where in opposition to ourselves.

Unaccustomed to reserve or mystery in the expression
of my opinions, I have opened myself frankly on a

question suggested by your letter and present. And although I have not the honor of your acquaintance, this mark of attention, and still more the sentiments of esteem so kindly expressed in your letter, are entitled to a confidence that observations not intended for the public will not be ushered to their notice, as has happened to me sometimes. Tranquillity, at my age, is the balm of life. While I know I am safe in the honor and charity of a McLeod, I do not wish to be cast forth to the Marats, the Dantons, and the Robespierres of the priesthood; I mean the Parishes, the Ogdens, and the Gardiners of Massachusetts.

I pray you to accept the assurances of my esteem and respect.

ANNUAL REPORT OF THE BOARD OF VISITORS OF THE UNIVERSITY OF VIRGINIA*

OCTOBER 7, 1822

. . . In the same report of the commissioners of 1818 it was stated by them that "in conformity with the principles of constitution, which place all sects of religion on an equal footing, with the jealousies of the different sects in guarding that equality from encroachment or surprise, and with the sentiments of the legislature in freedom of religion, manifested on former occasions, they had not proposed that any professorship of divinity should be established in the University; that provision, however, was made for giving instruction in the Hebrew, Greek and Latin languages, the depositories of the originals, and of the earliest and most respected authorities of the faith of every sect, and for courses of ethical lectures, developing those moral obligations in which all sects agree. That, proceeding thus far, without offence to the constitution, they had left, at this point, to every

* Saul K. Padover, *The Complete Jefferson* (New York: Tudor, 1943), pp. 957–58.

sect to take into their own hands the office of further
instruction in the peculiar tenet of each."

It was not, however, to be understood that instruction
in religious opinion and duties was meant to be precluded by the public authorities, as indifferent to the
interests of society. On the contrary, the relations which
exist between man and his Maker, and the duties resulting from those relations, are the most interesting and
important to every human being, and the most in-
cumbent on his study and investigation. The want of
instruction in the various creeds of religious faith existing among our citizens presents, therefore, a chasm in
a general institution of the useful sciences. But it was
thought that this want, and the entrustment to each
society of instruction in its own doctrine, were evils of
less danger than a permission to the public authorities
to dictate modes or principles of religious instruction,
or than opportunities furnished them by giving countenance or ascendancy to any one sect over another. A
remedy, however, has been suggested of promising aspect,
which, while it excludes the public authorities from the
domain of religious freedom, will give to the sectarian
schools of divinity the full benefit the public provisions
made for instruction in the other branches of science.
These branches are equally necessary to the divine as to
the other professional or civil characters, to enable them
to fulfill the duties of their calling with understanding
and usefulness. It has, therefore, been in contemplation,
and suggested by some pious individuals, who perceive
the advantages of associating other studies with those
of religion, to establish their religious schools on the
confines of the University, so as to give to their students
ready and convenient access and attendance on the
scientific lectures of the University; and to maintain,
by that means, those destined for the religious professions
on as high a standing of science, and of personal weight
and respectability, as may be obtained by others from
the benefits of the University. Such establishments would
offer the further and greater advantage of enabling the

students of the University to attend religious exercises with the professor of their particular sect, either in the rooms of the building still to be erected, and destined to that purpose under impartial regulations, as proposed in the same report of the commissioners, or in the lecturing room of such professor. To such propositions the Visitors are disposed to lend a willing ear, and would think it their duty to give every encouragement, by assuring to those who might choose such a location for their schools, that the regulations of the University should be so modified and accommodated as to give every facility of access and attendance to their students, with such regulated use also as may be permitted to the other students, of the library which may hereafter be acquired, either by public or private munificence. But always understanding that these schools shall be independent of the University and of each other. Such an arrangement would complete the circle of the useful sciences embraced by this institution, and would fill the chasm now existing, on principles which would leave inviolate the constitutional freedom of religion, the most inalienable and sacred of all human rights, over which the people and authorities of this state, individually and publicly, have ever manifested the most watchful jealousy: and could this jealousy be now alarmed, in the opinion of the legislature, by what is here suggested, the idea will be relinquished on any surmise of disapprobation which they might think proper to express. . . .

TO DOCTOR THOMAS COOPER*

Monticello, November 2, 1822.

DEAR SIR,—Your favor of October the 18th came to hand yesterday. The atmosphere of our country is unquestionably charged with a threatening cloud of fanaticism, lighter in some parts, denser in others, but too

* Ford, 10:242–44.

heavy in all. I had no idea, however, that in Pennsylvania, the cradle of toleration and freedom of religion, it could have arisen to the height you describe. This must be owing to the growth of Presbyterianism. The blasphemy and absurdity of the five points of Calvin, and the impossibility of defending them, render their advocates impatient of reasoning, irritable, and prone to denunciation. In Boston, however, and its neighborhood, Unitarianism has advanced to so great strength, as now to humble this haughtiest of all religious sects; insomuch that they condescend to interchange with them and the other sects, the civilities of preaching freely and frequently in each others' meeting-houses. In Rhode Island, on the other hand, no sectarian preacher will permit an Unitarian to pollute his desk. In our Richmond there is much fanaticism, but chiefly among the women. They have their night meetings and praying parties, where, attended by their priests, and sometimes by a hen-pecked husband, they pour forth the effusions of their love to Jesus, in terms as amatory and carnal, as their modesty would permit them to use to a mere earthly lover. In our village of Charlottesville, there is a good degree of religion, with a small spice only of fanaticism. We have four sects, but without either church or meeting-house. The court-house is the common temple, one Sunday in the month to each. Here, Episcopalian and Presbyterian, Methodist and Baptist, meet together, join in hymning their Maker, listen with attention and devotion to each others' preachers, and all mix in society with perfect harmony. It is not so in the districts where Presbyterianism prevails undividedly. Their ambition and tyranny would tolerate no rival if they had power. Systematical in grasping at an ascendency over all other sects, they aim, like the Jesuits, at engrossing the education of the country, are hostile to every institution which they do not direct, and jealous at seeing others begin to attend at all to that object. The diffusion of instruction, to which there is now so growing an attention, will be the remote remedy to this fever of fanaticism; while the more proximate one will be the progress of Unitarianism. That this will, ere long, be the religion of the majority from north to south, I have no doubt.

In our university you know there is no Professorship of Divinity. A handle has been made of this, to disseminate an idea that this is an institution, not merely of no religion, but against all religion. Occasion was taken at the last meeting of the Visitors, to bring forward an idea that might silence this calumny, which weighed on the minds of some honest friends to the institution. In our annual report to the legislature, after stating the constitutional reasons against a public establishment of any religious instruction, we suggest the expediency of encouraging the different religious sects to establish, each for itself, a professorship of their own tenets, on the confines of the university, so near as that their students may attend the lectures there, and have the free use of our library, and every other accommodation we can give them; preserving, however, their independence of us and of each other. This fills the chasm objected to ours, as a defect in an institution professing to give instruction in *all* useful sciences. I think the invitation will be accepted, by some sects from candid intentions, and by others from jealousy and rivalship. And by bringing the sects together, and mixing them with the mass of other students, we shall soften their asperities, liberalize and neutralize their prejudices, and make the general religion a religion of peace, reason, and morality.

The time of opening our university is still as uncertain as ever. All the pavilions, boarding houses, and dormitories are done. Nothing is now wanting but the central building for a library and other general purposes. For this we have no funds, and the last legislature refused all aid. We have better hopes of the next. But all is uncertain. I have heard with regret of disturbances on the part of the students in your seminary. The article of discipline is the most difficult in American education. Premature ideas of independence, too little repressed by parents, beget a spirit of insubordination, which is the great obstacle to science with us, and a principal cause of its decay since the revolution. I look to it with dismay in our institution, as a breaker ahead, which I am far from being confident we shall be able to weather. The advance of age, and tardy pace of the public patronage, may probably spare me the pain of witnessing consequences.

I salute you with constant friendship and respect.

3: The General Diffusion of Knowledge

"Where the press is free and every man able to read, all is safe."

Two interrelated misconceptions as to Jefferson's educational interests and accomplishments are often given currency. One of these is the allegation that Jefferson was really primarily concerned about the upper class and that his educational proposals were not genuinely democratic. The other misconception is the suggestion that Jefferson, as he grew older, became less liberal, more reactionary, with the result that his later views of school and college were far more aristocratic and restrictive in spirit than were the proposals of his earlier years. It is true that, during the years of his "retirement" after the presidency, Jefferson was both more active and more successful in his efforts to encourage higher education in Virginia than in the promotion of general schooling, which latter emphasis was so prominent in his activities during the 1770's and 1780's. But the fact is that throughout his life the entire process was a matter of the highest importance to him. "Nobody can doubt my zeal for the general instruction of the people," he wrote in 1821. "I never have proposed a sacrifice of the primary to the ultimate grade of instruction. Let us keep our eye steadily on the whole system." Both phases he regarded as crucial, and to understand the Jeffersonian design for education (to which let us apply Parrington's wonderful description of Jefferson himself: an "aristocratic head set on a plebeian frame") each—the primary school and the university—must be seen in its relation to the other.

81

The Bill for the More General Diffusion of Knowledge was one of three proposals emanating from the Committee of Revisors in 1779 which dealt with matters educational, the others being bills to amend the charter of the College of William and Mary and to establish a public library system. All three were drafted by Jefferson and, though none was adopted in its original form, they—and especially the first-named—constitute a very clear presentation of Jefferson's basic ideas on education. This educational outlook is further elaborated in the Notes on the State of Virginia *and in a host of letters, of which those to George Wythe and Edward Carrington included here are particularly cogent examples.*

Jefferson returned to the struggle for universal public education in 1817 when he drafted his second proposal for popular schooling for the consideration of the Virginia legislature. This was offered following the defeat of an earlier proposal which Jefferson had opposed as being fiscally unsound and overly centralized. In its provisions for primary education, Jefferson's bill of 1817 was not markedly different from that of 1779 (for which reason it is not reprinted here). Its significance lies in no small part in its demonstration of the constancy of Jefferson's central educational ideals in their relations to democratic government. But, taken together, the Jeffersonian suggestions for popular education stand as a monumental element in the American educational heritage. "In the light of history (writes Dumas Malone, 1:280–81), nothing else that he did or proposed during his entire career showed him more clearly to be a major American prophet."

SEE ALSO:

"A Bill for Amending the Constitution of the College of William and Mary, and Substituting More Certain Revenues for Its Support" [Revisal No. 80] (Boyd, 2:535–43).

"A Bill for Establishing a Public Library" [Revisal No. 81] (Boyd, 2:544–45).

Letter to Benjamin Banneker, August 30, 1791 (Ford, 5:377–78).

Letter to Joseph C. Cabell, February 2, 1816 (Honeywell, 228–29).

Letter to Joseph C. Cabell, September 9, 1817 (Lipscomb and Bergh, 17:417–18).

"A Bill for Establishing a System of Public Education," October 1817 (Honeywell, 233–43).

Letter to J. Correa de Serra, November 25, 1817 (Lipscomb and Bergh, 15:153–57).

Letter to George Ticknor, November 25, 1817 (Ford, 10:94–96).

Letter to Joseph C. Cabell, January 14, 1818 (Ford, 10:98–102).

Letter to Joseph C. Cabell, November 28, 1820 (Ford, 10:165–68).

A BILL FOR THE MORE GENERAL DIFFUSION OF KNOWLEDGE *

Whereas it appeareth that however certain forms of government are better calculated than others to protect individuals in the free exercise of their natural rights, and are at the same time themselves better guarded against degeneracy, yet experience hath shewn, that even under the best forms, those entrusted with power have, in time, and by slow operations, perverted it into tyranny; and it is believed that the most effectual means of preventing this would be, to illuminate, as far as practicable, the minds of the people at large, and more especially to give them knowledge of those facts, which history exhibiteth, that, possessed thereby of the experience of other ages and countries, they may be enabled to know ambition under all its shapes, and prompt to exert their natural powers to defeat its purposes; And whereas it is generally true that that people will be

* Julian P. Boyd, ed., *The Papers of Thomas Jefferson* (Princeton, N. J.: Princeton University Press, 1950 *et seq.*), 2:526–33.

happiest whose laws are best, and are best administered, and that laws will be wisely formed, and honestly administered, in proportion as those who form and administer them are wise and honest; whence it becomes expedient for promoting the publick happiness that those persons, whom nature hath endowed with genius and virtue, should be rendered by liberal education worthy to receive, and able to guard the sacred deposit of the rights and liberties of their fellow citizens, and that they should be called to that charge without regard to wealth, birth or other accidental condition or circumstance; but the indigence of the greater number disabling them from so educating, at their own expence, those of their children whom nature hath fitly formed and disposed to become useful instruments for the public, it is better that such should be sought for and educated at the common expence of all, than that the happiness of all should be confided to the weak or wicked:

Be it therefore enacted by the General Assembly, that in every county within this commonwealth, there shall be chosen annually, by the electors qualified to vote for Delegates, three of the most honest and able men of their county, to be called the Aldermen of the county; and that the election of the said Aldermen shall be held at the same time and place, before the same persons, and notified and conducted in the same manner as by law is directed for the annual election of Delegates for the county.

The person before whom such election is holden shall certify to the court of the said county the names of the Aldermen chosen, in order that the same may be entered of record, and shall give notice of their election to the said Aldermen within a fortnight after such election.

The said Aldermen on the first Monday in October, if it be fair, and if not, then on the next fair day, excluding Sunday, shall meet at the court-house of their county, and proceed to divide their said county into hundreds, bounding the same by water courses, mountains, or limits, to be run and marked, if they think necessary, by the county surveyor, and at the county expence, regulat-

ing the size of the said hundreds, according to the best
of their discretion, so as that they may contain a convenient number of children to make up a school, and
be of such convenient size that all the children within
each hundred may daily attend the school to be established therein, distinguishing each hundred by a particular name; which division, with the names of the several
hundreds, shall be returned to the court of the county
and be entered of record, and shall remain unaltered
until the increase or decrease of inhabitants shall render
an alteration necessary, in the opinion of any succeeding
Aldermen, and also in the opinion of the court of the
county.

The electors aforesaid residing within every hundred
shall meet on the third Monday in October after the
first election of Aldermen, at such place, within their
hundred, as the said Aldermen shall direct, notice thereof
being previously given to them by such person residing
within the hundred as the said Aldermen shall require
who is hereby enjoined to obey such requisition, on pain
of being punished by amercement and imprisonment.
The electors being so assembled shall choose the most
convenient place within their hundred for building a
school-house. If two or more places, having a greater
number of votes than any others, shall yet be equal between themselves, the Aldermen, or such of them as are
not of the same hundred, on information thereof, shall
decide between them. The said Aldermen shall forthwith
proceed to have a school-house built at the said place,
and shall see that the same be kept in repair, and, when
necessary, that it be rebuilt; but whenever they shall
think necessary that it be rebuilt, they shall give notice
as before directed, to the electors of the hundred to meet
at the said school-house, on such day as they shall appoint, to determine by vote, in the manner before
directed, whether it shall be rebuilt at the same, or
what other place in the hundred.

At every of these schools shall be taught reading, writing, and common arithmetick, and the books which shall
be used therein for instructing the children to read shall

be such as will at the same time make them acquainted with Græcian, Roman, English, and American history. At these schools all the free children, male and female, resident within the respective hundred, shall be intitled to receive tuition gratis, for the term of three years, and as much longer, at their private expence, as their parents, guardians or friends, shall think proper.

Over every ten of these schools (or such other number nearest thereto, as the number of hundreds in the county will admit, without fractional divisions) an overseer shall be appointed annually by the Aldermen at their first meeting, eminent for his learning, integrity, and fidelity to the commonwealth, whose business and duty it shall be, from time to time, to appoint a teacher to each school, who shall give assurance of fidelity to the commonwealth, and to remove him as he shall see cause; to visit every school once in every half year at the least; to examine the schollars; see that any general plan of reading and instruction recommended by the visiters of William and Mary College shall be observed; and to superintend the conduct of the teacher in every thing relative to his school.

Every teacher shall receive a salary of   by the year, which, with the expences of building and repairing the school-houses, shall be provided in such manner as other county expences are by law directed to be provided and shall also have his diet, lodging, and washing found him, to be levied in like manner, save only that such levy shall be on the inhabitants of each hundred for the board of their own teacher only.

And in order that grammar schools may be rendered convenient to the youth in every part of the commonwealth, Be it farther enacted, that on the first Monday in November, after the first appointment of overseers for the hundred schools, if fair, and if not, then on the next fair day, excluding Sunday, after the hour of one in the afternoon, the said overseers appointed for the schools in the counties of Princess Ann, Norfolk, Nansemond and Isle-of-Wight, shall meet at Nansemond court house; those for the counties of Southampton, Sussex, Surry and

Prince George, shall meet at Sussex court-house; those for the counties of Brunswick, Mecklenburg and Lunenburg, shall meet at Lunenburg court-house; those for the counties of Dinwiddie, Amelia and Chesterfield, shall meet at Chesterfield court-house; those for the counties of Powhatan, Cumberland, Goochland, Henrico and Hanover, shall meet at Henrico court-house; those for the counties of Prince Edward, Charlotte and Halifax, shall meet at Charlotte court-house; those for the counties of Henry, Pittsylvania and Bedford, shall meet at Pittsylvania court-house; those for the counties of Buckingham, Amherst, Albemarle and Fluvanna, shall meet at Albemarle court-house; those for the counties of Botetourt, Rockbridge, Montgomery, Washington and Kentucky, shall meet at Botetourt court-house; those for the counties of Augusta, Rockingham and Greenbrier, shall meet at Augusta court-house; those for the counties of Accomack and Northampton, shall meet at Accomack court-house; those for the counties of Elizabeth City, Warwick, York, Gloucester, James City, Charles City and New-Kent, shall meet at James City court-house; those for the counties of Middlesex, Essex, King and Queen, King William and Caroline, shall meet at King and Queen court-house; those for the counties of Lancaster, Northumberland, Richmond and Westmoreland, shall meet at Richmond court-house; those for the counties of King George, Stafford, Spotsylvania, Prince William and Fairfax, shall meet at Spotsylvania court-house; those for the counties of Loudoun and Fauquier, shall meet at Loudoun court-house; those for the counties of Culpeper, Orange and Louisa, shall meet at Orange court-house; those for the counties of Shenandoah and Frederick, shall meet at Frederick court-house; those for the counties of Hampshire and Berkeley, shall meet at Berkeley court-house; and those for the counties of Yohogania, Monongalia and Ohio, shall meet at Monongalia court-house; and shall fix on such place in some one of the counties in their district as shall be most proper for situating a grammar school-house, endeavouring that the situation be as central as may be to the inhabitants of the said counties, that it be furnished with good water, convenient to plentiful supplies of provision and fuel, and more than all things that it be healthy. And if a majority of the overseers present should not concur in their choice of any one place proposed, the method of determining shall be as follows: If two places only were proposed, and the votes be divided, they shall decide between them by fair and equal lot; if more than two places were proposed, the question shall be put on those two which on the first division had the greater number of votes; or if no two places had a greater number of votes than the others, as where the votes shall have been equal between one or both of them and some other or others, then it shall be decided by fair and equal lot (unless it can be agreed by a majority of votes) which of the places having equal numbers shall be thrown out of the competition, so that the question shall be put on the remaining two, and if on this ultimate question the votes shall be equally divided, it shall then be decided finally by lot.

The said overseers having determined the place at which the grammar school for their district shall be built, shall forthwith (unless they can otherwise agree with the proprietors of the circumjacent lands as to location and price) make application to the clerk of the county in which the said house is to be situated, who shall thereupon issue a writ, in the nature of a writ of ad quod damnum, directed to the sheriff of the said county commanding him to summon and impannel twelve fit persons to meet at the place, so destined for the grammar school house, on a certain day, to be named in the said writ, not less than five, nor more than ten, days from the date thereof; and also to give notice of the same to the proprietors and tenants of the lands to be viewed, if they be to be found within the county, and if not, then to their agents therein if any they have. Which freeholders shall be charged by the said sheriff impartially, and to the best of their skill and judgment to view the lands round about the said place, and to locate and circumscribe, by certain metes and bounds, one hun-

dred acres thereof, having regard therein principally
to the benefit and convenience of the said school,
but respecting in some measure also the convenience
of the said proprietors, and to value and appraise the
same in so many several and distinct parcels as shall
be owned or held by several and distinct owners or
tenants, and according to their respective interests and
estates therein. And after such location and appraise-
ment so made, the said sheriff shall forthwith return
the same under the hands and seals of the said jurors,
together with the writ, to the clerk's office of the said
county and the right and property of the said proprietors and tenants in the said lands so circumscribed
shall be immediately devested and be transferred to
the commonwealth for the use of the said grammar
school, in full and absolute dominion, any want of
consent or disability to consent in the said owners
or tenants notwithstanding. But it shall not be lawful
for the said overseers so to situate the said grammar
school-house, nor to the said jurors so to locate the said
lands, as to include the mansion-house of the proprietor
of the lands, nor the offices, curtilage, or garden, there-
unto immediately belonging.

The said overseers shall forthwith proceed to have a
house of brick or stone, for the said grammar school,
with necessary offices, built on the said lands, which
grammar school-house shall contain a room for the
school, a hall to dine in, four rooms for a master and
usher, and ten or twelve lodging rooms for the scholars.

To each of the said grammar schools shall be allowed
out of the public treasury, the sum of   pounds,
out of which shall be paid by the Treasurer, on warrant
from the Auditors, to the proprietors or tenants of the
lands located, the value of their several interests as fixed
by the jury, and the balance thereof shall be delivered
to the said overseers to defray the expence of the said
buildings.

In these grammar schools shall be taught the Latin
and Greek languages, English grammar, geography, and
the higher part of numerical arithmetick, to wit, vulgar

and decimal fractions, and the extraction of the square and cube roots.

A visiter from each county constituting the district shall be appointed, by the overseers, for the county, in the month of October annually, either from their own body or from their county at large, which visiters or the greater part of them, meeting together at the said grammar school on the first Monday in November, if fair, and if not, then on the next fair day, excluding Sunday, shall have power to choose their own Rector, who shall call and preside at future meetings, to employ from time to time a master, and if necessary, an usher, for the said school, to remove them at their will, and to settle the price of tuition to be paid by the scholars. They shall also visit the school twice in every year at the least, either together or separately at their discretion, examine the scholars, and see that any general plan of instruction recommended by the visiters of William and Mary College shall be observed. The said masters and ushers, before they enter on the execution of their office, shall give assurance of fidelity to the commonwealth.

A steward shall be employed, and removed at will by the master, on such wages as the visiters shall direct; which steward shall see to the procuring provisions, fuel, servants for cooking, waiting, house cleaning, washing, mending, and gardening on the most reasonable terms; the expence of which, together with the steward's wages, shall be divided equally among all the scholars boarding either on the public or private expence. And the part of those who are on private expence, and also the price of their tuitions due to the master or usher, shall be paid quarterly by the respective scholars, their parents, or guardians, and shall be recoverable, if withheld, together with costs, on motion in any Court of Record, ten days notice thereof being previously given to the party, and a jury impannelled to try the issue joined, or enquire of the damages. The said steward shall also, under the direction of the visiters, see that the houses be kept in repair, and necessary enclosures be made and repaired, the accounts for which, shall, from time to time, be submitted to the Auditors, and on their warrant paid by the Treasurer.

Every overseer of the hundred schools shall, in the month of September annually, after the most diligent and impartial examination and enquiry, appoint from among the boys who shall have been two years at the least at some one of the schools under his superintendance, and whose parents are too poor to give them farther education, some one of the best and most promising genius and disposition, to proceed to the grammar school of his district; which appointment shall be made in the court-house of the county, on the court day for that month if fair, and if not, then on the next fair day, excluding Sunday, in the presence of the Aldermen, or two of them at the least, assembled on the bench for that purpose, the said overseer being previously sworn by them to make such appointment, without favor or affection, according to the best of his skill and judgment, and being interrogated by the said Aldermen, either on their own motion, or on suggestions from the parents, guardians, friends, or teachers of the children, competitors for such appointment; which teachers shall attend for the information of the Aldermen. On which interregatories the said Aldermen, if they be not satisfied with the appointment proposed, shall have right to negative it; whereupon the said visiter may proceed to make a new appointment, and the said Aldermen again to interrogate and negative, and so toties quoties until an appointment be approved.

Every boy so appointed shall be authorised to proceed to the grammar school of his district, there to be educated and boarded during such time as is hereafter limited; and his quota of the expences of the house together with a compensation to the master or usher for his tuition, at the rate of twenty dollars by the year, shall be paid by the Treasurer quarterly on warrant from the Auditors.

A visitation shall be held, for the purpose of probation, annually at the said grammar school on the last Monday in September, if fair, and if not, then on the

next fair day, excluding Sunday, at which one third of
the boys sent thither by appointment of the said overseers, and who shall have been there one year only,
shall be discontinued as public foundationers, being
those who, on the most diligent examination and enquiry, shall be thought to be of the least promising
genius and disposition; and of those who shall have been
there two years, all shall be discontinued, save one only
the best in genius and disposition, who shall be at liberty
to continue there four years longer on the public foundation, and shall thence forward be deemed a senior.

The visiters for the districts which, or any part of
which, be southward and westward of James river, as
known by that name, or by the names of Fluvanna and
Jackson's river, in every other year, to wit, at the probation meetings held in the years, distinguished in the
Christian computation by odd numbers, and the visiters
for all the other districts at their said meetings to be held
in those years, distinguished by even numbers, after diligent examination and enquiry as before directed, shall
chuse one among the said seniors, of the best learning
and most hopeful genius and disposition, who shall be
authorised by them to proceed to William and Mary
College, there to be educated, boarded, and clothed,
three years; the expence of which annually shall be paid
by the Treasurer on warrant from the Auditors.

NOTES ON THE STATE OF VIRGINIA*

QUERY XIV.

The administration of justice and the description of the laws?

... Many of the laws which were in force during the
monarchy being relative merely to that form of government, or inculcating principles inconsistent with republicanism, the first assembly which met after the establish-

* Paul L. Ford, ed., *The Writings of Thomas Jefferson* (New York: G. P. Putnam's Sons, 1892–1899), 3:242–43, 250–55.

ment of the commonwealth, appointed a committee to revise the whole code, to reduce it into proper form and volume, and report it to the assembly. This work has been executed by three gentlemen, and reported; but probably will not be taken up till a restoration of peace shall leave to the legislature leisure to go through such a work.

The plan of the revisal was this. The common law of England, by which is meant that part of the English law which was anterior to the date of the oldest statutes extant, is made the basis of the work. It was thought dangerous to attempt to reduce it to a text: it was therefore left to be collected from the usual monuments of it. Necessary alterations in that, and so much of the whole body of the British statutes, and of acts of assembly, as were thought proper to be retained, were digested into 126 new acts, in which simplicity of style was aimed at, as far as was safe. The following are the most remarkable alterations proposed:

To change the rules of descent, so as that the lands of any person dying intestate shall be divisible equally among all his children, or other representatives, in equal degree.

To make slaves distributable among the next of kin, as other movables.

To have all public expences, whether of the general treasury, or of a parish or county, (as for the maintenance of the poor, building bridges, court-houses, &c.,) supplied by assessments on the citizens, in proportion to their property.

To hire undertakers for keeping the public roads in repair, and indemnify individuals through whose lands new roads shall be opened.

To define with precision the rules whereby aliens should become citizens, and citizens make themselves aliens.

To establish religious freedom on the broadest bottom.

To emancipate all slaves born after passing the act. . . .

The revised code further proposes to proportion crimes and punishments. . . .

Another object of the revisal is, to diffuse knowledge more generally through the mass of the people. This bill proposes to lay off every county into small districts of five or six miles square, called hundreds and in each of them to establish a school for teaching, reading, writing, and arithmetic. The tutor to be supported by the hundred, and every person in it entitled to send their children three years gratis, and as much longer as they please, paying for it. These schools to be under a visitor who is annually to chuse the boy of best genius in the school, of those whose parents are too poor to give them further education, and to send him forward to one of the grammar schools, of which twenty are proposed to be erected in different parts of the country, for teaching Greek, Latin, geography, and the higher branches of numerical arithmetic. Of the boys thus sent in any one year, trial is to be made at the grammar schools one or two years, and the best genius of the whole selected, and continued six years, and the residue dismissed. By this means twenty of the best geniuses will be raked from the rubbish annually, and be instructed, at the public expence, so far as the grammar schools go. At the end of six years instruction, one half are to be discontinued (from among whom the grammar schools will probably be supplied with future masters); and the other half, who are to be chosen for the superiority of their parts and disposition, are to be sent and continued three years in the study of such sciences as they shall chuse, at William and Mary college, the plan of which is proposed to be enlarged, as will be hereafter explained, and extended to all the useful sciences. The ultimate result of the whole scheme of education would be the teaching all the children of the State reading, writing, and common arithmetic; turning out ten annually, of superior genius, well taught in Greek, Latin, geography, and the higher branches of arithmetic; turning out ten others annually, of still superior parts, who, to those branches of learning, shall have added such of the sciences as their genius shall have led them to; the furnishing to the wealthier part of the people convenient schools at which their children may be edu-

cated at their own expence.—The general objects of this
law are to provide an education adapted to the years, to
the capacity, and the condition of every one, and directed to their freedom and happiness. Specific details
were not proper for the law. These must be the business
of the visitors entrusted with its execution. The first
stage of this education being the schools of the hundreds,
wherein the great mass of the people will receive their
instruction, the principal foundations of future order
will be laid here. Instead, therefore, of putting the Bible
and Testament into the hands of the children at an age
when their judgments are not sufficiently matured for
religious inquiries, their memories may here be stored
with the most useful facts from Grecian, Roman, European, and American history. The first elements of morality too may be instilled into their minds; such as, when
further developed as their judgments advance in strength,
may teach them how to work out their own greatest
happiness, by shewing them that it does not depend on
the condition of life in which chance has placed them,
but is always the result of a good conscience, good health,
occupation, and freedom in all just pursuits.—Those
whom either the wealth of their parents or the adoption
of the state shall destine to higher degrees of learning,
will go on to the grammar schools, which constitute the
next stage, there to be instructed in the languages. The
learning Greek and Latin, I am told, is going into disuse
in Europe. I know not what their manners and occupations may call for: but it would be very ill-judged in us
to follow their example in this instance. There is a certain period of life, say from eight to fifteen or sixteen
years of age, when the mind like the body is not yet firm
enough for laborious and close operations. If applied to
such, it falls an early victim to premature exertion; ex-
hibiting, indeed, at first, in these young and tender subjects, the flattering appearance of their being men while
they are yet children, but ending in reducing them to be
children when they should be men. The memory is then
most susceptible and tenacious of impressions; and the
learning of languages being chiefly a work of memory,

it seems precisely fitted to the powers of this period, which is long enough too for acquiring the most useful languages, antient and modern. I do not pretend that language is science. It is only an instrument for the attainment of science. But that time is not lost which is employed in providing tools for future operation: more especially as in this case the books put into the hands of the youth for this purpose may be such as will at the same time impress their minds with useful facts and good principles. If this period be suffered to pass in idleness, the mind becomes lethargic and impotent, as would the body it inhabits if unexercised during the same time. The sympathy between body and mind during their rise, progress and decline, is too strict and obvious to endanger our being misled while we reason from the one to the other.—As soon as they are of sufficient age, it is supposed they will be sent on from the grammar schools to the university, which constitutes our third and last stage, there to study those sciences which may be adapted to their views.—By that part of our plan which prescribes the selection of the youths of genius from among the classes of the poor, we hope to avail the state of those talents which nature has sown as liberally among the poor as the rich, but which perish without use, if not sought for and cultivated.—But of all the views of this law none is more important, none more legitimate, than that of rendering the people the safe, as they are the ultimate, guardians of their own liberty. For this purpose the reading in the first stage, where *they* will receive their whole education, is proposed, as has been said, to be chiefly historical. History, by apprising them of the past, will enable them to judge of the future; it will avail them of the experience of other times and other nations; it will qualify them as judges of the actions and designs of men; it will enable them to know ambition under every disguise it may assume; and knowing it, to defeat its views. In every government on earth is some trace of human weakness, some germ of corruption and degeneracy, which cunning will discover, and wickedness insensibly open, cultivate and improve. Every government degenerates when trusted to the rulers of the people alone. The people themselves therefore are its only safe depositories. And to render even them safe, their minds must be improved to a certain degree. This indeed is not all that is necessary, though it be essentially necessary. An amendment of our constitution must here come in aid of the public education. The influence over government must be shared among all the people. If every individual which composes their mass participates of the ultimate authority, the government will be safe; because the corrupting the whole mass will exceed any private resources of wealth; and public ones cannot be provided but by levies on the people. In this case every man would have to pay his own price. The government of Great Britain has been corrupted, because but one man in ten has a right to vote for members of parliament. The sellers of the government, therefore, get nine-tenths of their price clear. It has been thought that corruption is restrained by confining the right of suffrage to a few of the wealthier of the people: but it would be more effectually restrained by an extension of that right to such numbers as would bid defiance to the means of corruption.

Lastly, it is proposed, by a bill in this revisal, to begin a public library and gallery, by laying out a certain sum annually in books, paintings, and statues. . . .

TO GEORGE WYTHE*

DEAR SIR   Paris Aug. 13. 1786.

Your favors of Jan. 10. and Feb. 10. came to hand on the 20th. and 23d of May. I availed myself of the first opportunity which occurred, by a gentleman going to England, of sending to Mr. Joddrel a copy of the Notes on our country, with a line informing him that it was you who had emboldened me to take that liberty. Madi-

* Boyd, 10:243-45.

son, no doubt, informed you of the reason why I had sent only a single copy to Virginia. Being assured by him that they will not do the harm I had apprehended, but on the contrary may do some good, I propose to send thither the copies remaining on hand, which are fewer than I had intended, but of the numerous corrections they need, there are one or two so essential that I must have them made, by printing a few new leaves and substituting them for the old. This will be done while they are engraving a map which I have constructed of the country from Albemarle sound to Lake Erie, and which will be inserted in the book. A bad French translation which is getting out here, will probably oblige me to publish the original more freely, which it neither deserved nor was ever intended. Your wishes, which are laws to me, will justify my destining a copy for you. Otherwise I should as soon have thought of sending you a horn-book; for there is no truth there that is not familiar to you, and it's errors I should hardly have proposed to treat you with.

Immediately on the receipt of your letter, I wrote to a correspondent at Florence to enquire after the family of Tagliaferro as you desired. I received his answer two days ago, a copy of which I now inclose. The original shall be sent by some other occasion. I will have the copper plate immediately engraved. This may be ready within a few days, but the probability is that I shall be long getting an opportunity of sending it to you, as these rarely occur. You do not mention the size of the plate but, presuming it is intended for labels for the inside of books, I shall have it made of a proper size for that. I shall omit the word $\alpha\rho\iota\sigma\sigma$, according to the license you allow me, because I think the beauty of a motto is to condense much matter in as few words as possible. The word omitted will be supplied by every reader.

The European papers have announced that the assembly of Virginia were occupied on the revisal of their Code of laws. This, with some other similar intelligence, has contributed much to convince the people of Europe, that what the English papers are constantly publishing of our anarchy, is false; as they are sensible that such a work is that of a people only who are in perfect tranquillity. Our act for freedom of religion is extremely applauded. The Ambassadors and ministers of the several nations of Europe resident at this court have asked of me copies of it to send to their sovereigns, and it is inserted at full length in several books now in the press; among others, in the new Encyclopedie. I think it will produce considerable good even in these countries where ignorance, superstition, poverty and oppression of body and mind in every form, are so firmly settled on the mass of the people, that their redemption from them can never be hoped. If the almighty had begotten a thousand sons, instead of one, they would not have sufficed for this task. If all the sovereigns of Europe were to set themselves to work to emancipate the minds of their subjects from their present ignorance and prejudices, and that as zealously as they now endeavor the contrary, a thousand years would not place them on that high ground on which our common people are now setting out. Ours could not have been so fairly put into the hands of their own common sense, had they not been separated from their parent stock and been kept from contamination, either from them, or the other people of the old world, by the intervention of so wide an ocean. To know the worth of this, one must see the want of it here. I think by far the most important bill in our whole code is that for the diffusion of knowledge among the people. No other sure foundation can be devised for the preservation of freedom, and happiness. If any body thinks that kings, nobles, or priests are good conservators of the public happiness, send them here. It is the best school in the universe to cure them of that folly. They will see here with their own eyes that these descriptions of men are an abandoned confederacy against the happiness of the mass of people. The omnipotence of their effect cannot be better proved than in this country particularly, where notwithstanding the finest soil upon earth, the finest climate under heaven, and a people of the most benevolent, the most gay, and amiable character of which the human form is susceptible, where such a people I say, surrounded by so many blessings from nature, are yet loaded with misery by kings, nobles and priests, and by them alone. Preach, my dear Sir, a crusade against ignorance; establish and improve the law for educating the common people. Let our countrymen know that the people alone can protect us against these evils, and that the tax which will be paid for this purpose is not more than the thousandth part of what will be paid to kings, priests and nobles who will rise up among us if we leave the people in ignorance.—The people of England, I think, are less oppressed than here. But it needs but half an eye to see, when among them, that the foundation is laid in their dispositions, for the establishment of a despotism. Nobility, wealth, and pomp are the objects of their adoration. They are by no means the free-minded people we suppose them in America. Their learned men too are few in number, and are less learned and infinitely less emancipated from prejudice than those of this country. An event too seems to be prospering, in the order of things, which will probably decide the fate of that country. It is no longer doubtful that the harbour of Cherbourg will be completed, that it will be a most excellent one, and capacious enough to hold the whole navy of France. Nothing has ever been wanting to enable this country to invade that, but a naval force conveniently stationed to protect the transports. This change of situation, must oblige the English to keep up a great standing army, and there is no king, who, with a sufficient force, is not always ready to make himself absolute.—My paper warns me it is time to recommend myself to the friendly recollection of Mrs. Wythe, of Colo. Taliaferro and his family and particularly of Mr. R. T. and to assure you of the affectionate esteem with which I am Dear Sir your friend & servt.,

TH: JEFFERSON

TO EDWARD CARRINGTON*

DEAR SIR   Paris Jan. 16. 1787.

Incertain whether you might be at New York at the
moment of Colo. Franks's arrival, I have inclosed my
private letters for Virginia under cover to our delegation
in general, which otherwise I would have taken the
liberty to inclose particularly to you, as best acquainted
with the situation of the persons to whom they are addressed. Should this find you at New York, I will still
ask your attention to them. The two large packages addressed to Colo. N. Lewis contain seeds, not valuable
enough to pay postage, but which I would wish to be
sent by the stage, or any similar quick conveyance. The
letters to Colo. Lewis and Mr. Eppes (who take care of
my affairs) are particularly interesting to me. The pack-
age for Colo. Richd. Cary our judge of Admiralty near
Hampton, contains seeds and roots, not to be sent by
post. Whether they had better go by the stage, or by
water, you will be the best judge. I beg your pardon for
giving you this trouble. But my situation and your good-
ness will I hope excuse it.

In my letter to Mr. Jay I have mentioned the meeting
of the Notables appointed for the 29th. inst. It is now
put off to the 7th. or 8th. of next month. This event,
which will hardly excite any attention in America, is
deemed here the most important one which has taken
place in their civil line during the present century. Some
promise their country great things from it, some nothing.
Our friend de la fayette was placed on the list originally.
Afterwards his name disappeared: but finally was rein-
stated. This shews that his character here is not considered as an indifferent one; and that it excites agitation. His education in our school has drawn on him a
very jealous eye from a court whose principles are the
most absolute despotism. But I hope he has nearly passed

* Boyd, 11:48–50.

his crisis. The king, who is a good man, is favorably disposed towards him: and he is supported by powerful family connections, and by the public good will. He is the youngest man of the Notables, except one whose office placed him on the list.

The Count de Vergennes has within these ten days had a very severe attack of what is deemed an unfixed gout. He has been well enough however to do business to-day. But anxieties for him are not yet quieted. He is a great and good minister, and an accident to him might endanger the peace of Europe.

The tumults in America, I expected would have produced in Europe an unfavorable opinion of our political state. But it has not. On the contrary, the small effect of those tumults seems to have given more confidence in the firmness of our governments. The interposition of the people themselves on the side of government has had a great effect on the opinion here. I am persuaded myself that the good sense of the people will always be found to be the best army. They may be led astray for a moment, but will soon correct themselves. The people are the only censors of their governors: and even their errors will tend to keep these to the true principles of their institution. To punish these errors too severely would be to suppress the only safeguard of the public liberty. The way to prevent these irregular interpositions of the people is to give them full information of their affairs thro' the channel of the public papers, and to contrive that those papers should penetrate the whole mass of the people. The basis of our governments being the opinion of the people, the very first object should be to keep that right; and were it left to me to decide whether we should have a government without newspapers, or newspapers without a government, I should not hesitate a moment to prefer the latter. But I should mean that every man should receive those papers and be capable of reading them. I am convinced that those societies (as the Indians) which live without government enjoy in their general mass an infinitely greater degree of happiness than those who live under European governments. Among the former, public opinion is in the place of law, and restrains morals as powerfully as laws ever did any where. Among the latter, under pretence of governing they have divided their nations into two classes, wolves and sheep. I do not exaggerate. This is a true picture of Europe. Cherish therefore the spirit of our people, and keep alive their attention. Do not be too severe upon their errors, but reclaim them by enlightening them. If once they become inattentive to the public affairs, you and I, and Congress, and Assemblies, judges and governors shall all become wolves. It seems to be the law of our general nature, in spite of individual exceptions; and experience declares that man is the only animal which devours his own kind, for I can apply no milder term to the governments of Europe, and to the general prey of the rich on the poor.—The want of news has led me into disquisition instead of narration, forgetting you have every day enough of that. I shall be happy to hear from you some times, only observing that whatever passes thro' the post is read, and that when you write what should be read by myself only, you must be so good as to confide your letter to some passenger or officer of the packet. I will ask your permission to write to you sometimes, and to assure you of the esteem & respect with which I have the honour to be Dear Sir your most obedient & most humble servt.,

TH: JEFFERSON

4: The Useful Sciences
in Their Highest Degree

> ". . . that man may be governed by reason
> and truth."

*There is a sense in which Jefferson may be said to come
to life most vividly when he is seen at work on the advancement of higher education. It may be that while
popular education was uppermost in his Head, the university and higher learning were really closest to his
Heart. Both for its social utility and for its own sake, the
advancement of science seemed to him man's sublimest
activity, and the promotion of institutions to that end
was to him perhaps the most exciting of his many pursuits.*

*As has been suggested, Jefferson was truly the "father"
of the University of Virginia for it was he who, far beyond any others, moved his state to found the institution. It is clear that his recommendations of 1779 for
the reform of William and Mary College really amounted
to a call for a state university and his efforts to reform
the college while governor of Virginia indicate his eagerness to broaden its serviceability to the entire commonwealth. The letters to John Bannister and John Adams
in this section suggest something of his conception of
what should characterize higher education in the young
republic. In the letter to George Ticknor we are advised
of the conversion of Albemarle Academy in Charlottesville into Central College, this in turn destined to be the
foundation for the University of Virginia. It is intriguing
to call to mind, as backdrop for this letter, the picture of
Jefferson, Madison, and Monroe, all members of the
Board of Visitors of Central College, quietly meeting to*

plan a campaign for making the tiny infant college the precursor of the state's first university. Was ever an institution more auspiciously sponsored?

When the legislature, as noted earlier, rejected Jefferson's Education Bill of 1817, a meager program of primary schools for the poor was authorized. To this bill as passed by the lower chamber, however, the Senate forced the addition of an amendment granting at least a token provision for higher education. "Thus (says Honeywell), engrafted upon a bill for the education of the poor, and wrung from a democratic House by a conservative Senate, began the University of Virginia." The "Rockfish Gap" report here reproduced, which was the direct result of that legislation, was accepted almost verbatim in the form in which it had been written by Jefferson. From it, under the zealous supervision of the "Old Sachem," as Jefferson was affectionately called by his closest associates in the venture, emerged the noble university in Charlottesville.

As the university's first Rector and chairman of its Board of Visitors, Jefferson continued to shape the newborn institution. Its architecture, its library, its faculty, its rules and regulations, its curriculum—all came under his loving scrutiny. With respect to the last, his concern for the maintenance of republican political principles moved him, as indicated by the letter to Joseph C. Cabell (after Jefferson, foremost among the founders of the university) and the minutes of the Board included in this section, to insist upon one explicit prescription in the course of study. Some will argue that here Jefferson woefully contradicted himself. But others will see in this a measure essential to the very survival of the democratic way and of genuine academic freedom. Jefferson's faith in the university as the "chief bulwark of the human mind" in a free society is typified by his eloquent words to William B. Giles penned just six months before his death.

SEE ALSO:

"A Bill for Amending the Constitution of the College of William and Mary, and Substituting More Certain

Revenues for Its Support" [Revisal No. 80] (Boyd, 2:535–43).

"A Bill for Establishing a Public Library" [Revisal No. 81] (Boyd, 2:544–45).

Letter to Joseph Priestley, January 18, 1800 (Ford, 7:406–10).

Letter to Joseph Priestley, January 27, 1800 (Ford, 7:413–16).

Letter to Judge John Tyler, June 28, 1804 (Koch-Peden, 576–77).

Letter to Peter Carr, September 7, 1814 (Koch-Peden, 642–49).

Letter to John Brazier, August 24, 1819 (Lipscomb and Bergh, 15:207–11).

Letter to William Roscoe, December 27, 1820 (Koch-Peden, 702).

"Regulations Adopted by the Board of Visitors of the University of Virginia, April 7, 1824" (Padover, 1106–11).

TO JOHN BANISTER, JR.*

DEAR SIR   Paris Oct. 15. 1785.

I should sooner have answered the paragraph in your favor of Sep. 19. respecting the best seminary for the education of youth in Europe, but that it was necessary for me to make enquiries on the subject. The result of these has been to consider the competition as resting between Geneva and Rome. They are equally cheap, and probably are equal in the course of education pursued. The advantage of Geneva is that students acquire there the habits of speaking French. The advantages of Rome are the acquiring a local knowledge of a spot so classical and so celebrated; the acquiring the true pronuntiation of the Latin language; the acquiring a just taste in the fine arts, more particularly those of painting, sculpture, Architecture, and Music;

* Julian P. Boyd, ed., *The Papers of Thomas Jefferson* (Princeton, N. J.: Princeton University Press, 1950 *et seq.*), 8:635–37.

a familiarity with those objects and processes of agriculture which experience has shewn best adapted to a climate like ours; and lastly the advantage of a fine climate for health. It is probable too that by being boarded in a French family the habit of speaking that language may be obtained. I do not count on any advantage to be derived in Geneva from a familiar acquaintance with the principles of it's government. The late revolution has rendered it a tyrannical aristocracy more likely to give ill than good ideas to an American. I think the balance in favor of Rome. Pisa is sometimes spoken of as a place of education. But it does not offer the 1st. and 3d. of the advantages of Rome. But why send an American youth to Europe for education? What are the objects of an useful American education? Classical knowlege, modern languages and chiefly French, Spanish, and Italian; Mathematics; Natural philosophy; Natural History; Civil History; Ethics. In Natural philosophy I mean to include Chemistry and Agriculture, and in Natural history to include Botany as well as the other branches of those departments. It is true that the habit of speaking the modern languages cannot be so well acquired in America, but every other article can be as well acquired at William and Mary College as at any place in Europe. When College education is done with and a young man is to prepare himself for public life, he must cast his eyes (for America) either on Law or Physic. For the former where can he apply so advantageously as to Mr. Wythe? For the latter he must come to Europe; the medical class of students therefore is the only one which need come to Europe. Let us view the disadvantages of sending a youth to Europe. To enumerate them all would require a volume. I will select a few. If he goes to England he learns drinking, horse-racing and boxing. These are the peculiarities of English education. The following circumstances are common to education in that and the other countries of Europe. He acquires a fondness for European luxury and dissipation and a contempt for the simplicity of his own country; he is fascinated with the privileges of the European aristocrats, and sees with abhorrence the lovely equality which the poor enjoys with the rich in his own country: he contracts a partiality for aristocracy or monarchy; he forms foreign friendships which will never be useful to him, and loses the season of life for forming in his own country those friendships which of all others are the most faithful and permanent: he is led by the strongest of all human passions into a spirit for female intrigue destructive of his own and others happiness, or a passion for whores destructive of his health, and in both cases learns to consider fidelity to the marriage bed as an ungentlemanly practice and inconsistent with happiness: he recollects the voluptuary dress and arts of the European women and pities and despises the chaste affections and simplicity of those of his own country; he retains thro' life a fond recollection and a hankering after those places which were the scenes of his first pleasures and of his first connections; he returns to his own country, a foreigner, unacquainted with the practices of domestic œconomy necessary to preserve him from ruin; speaking and writing his native tongue as a foreigner, and therefore unqualified to obtain those distinctions which eloquence of the pen and tongue ensures in a free country; for I would observe to you that what is called style in writing or speaking is formed very early in life while the imagination is warm, and impressions are permanent. I am of opinion that there never was an instance of a man's writing or speaking his native tongue with elegance who passed from 15. to 20. years of age out of the country where it was spoken. Thus no instance exists of a person writing two languages perfectly. That will always appear to be his native language which was most familiar to him in his youth. It appears to me then that an American coming to Europe for education loses in his knowlege, in his morals, in his health, in his habits, and in his happiness. I had entertained only doubts on this head before I came to Europe: what I see and hear since I come here proves more than I had even suspected. Cast your eye over America: who are the men of most learning, of most eloquence, most beloved by their country and most trusted and promoted by them? They are those who have been educated among them, and whose manners, morals and habits are perfectly homogeneous with those of the country.— Did you expect by so short a question to draw such a sermon on yourself? I dare say you did not. But the consequences of foreign education are alarming to me as an American. I sin therefore through zeal whenever I enter on the subject. You are sufficiently American to pardon me for it. Let me hear of your health and be assured of the esteem with which I am Dear Sir Your friend & servant,

TH: JEFFERSON

TO JOHN ADAMS*

Monticello, July 5, 1814

... I am just returned from one of my long absences, having been at my other home for five weeks past. Having more leisure there than here for reading, I amused myself with reading seriously Plato's Republic. I am wrong, however, in calling it amusement, for it was the heaviest task-work I ever went through. I had occasionally before taken up some of his other works, but scarcely ever had patience to go through a whole dialogue. While wading through the whimsies, the puerilities, and unintelligible jargon of this work, I laid it down often to ask myself how it could have been, that the world should have so long consented to give reputation to such nonsense as this? How the *soi-disant* Christian world, indeed, should have done it, is a piece of historical curiosity. But how could the Roman good sense do it? And particularly, how could Cicero bestow such eulogies on Plato! Although Cicero did not wield the dense logic of Demosthenes,

* Paul L. Ford, ed., *The Writings of Thomas Jefferson* (New York: G. P. Putnam's Sons, 1892–1899), 9:462–65.

yet he was able, learned, laborious, practised in the
business of the world, and honest. He could not be the
dupe of mere style, of which he was himself the first
master in the world. With the moderns, I think, it is
rather a matter of fashion and authority. Education
is chiefly in the hands of persons who, from their profession, have an interest in the reputation and the dreams
of Plato. They give the tone while at school, and few
in their after years have occasion to revise their college
opinions. But fashion and authority apart, and bringing
Plato to the test of reason, take from him his sophisms,
futilities and incomprehensibilities, and what remains?
In truth, he is one of the race of genuine sophists,
who has escaped the oblivion of his brethren, first,
by the elegance of his diction, but chiefly, by the adoption and incorporation of his whimsies into the body
of artificial Christianity. His foggy mind is forever
presenting the semblances of objects which, half seen
through a mist, can be defined neither in form nor di-
mensions. Yet this, which should have consigned him
to early oblivion, really procured him immortality of
fame and reverence. The Christian priesthood, finding
the doctrines of Christ levelled to every understanding,
and too plain to need explanation, saw in the mysticism
of Plato materials with which they might build up an
artificial system, which might, from its indistinctness,
admit everlasting controversy, give employment for their
order, and introduce it to profit, power and pre-emi-
nence. The doctrines which flowed from the lips of
Jesus himself are within the comprehension of a child;
but thousands of volumes have not yet explained the
Platonisms engrafted on them; and for this obvious
reason, that nonsense can never be explained. Their
purposes, however, are answered. Plato is canonized;
and it is now deemed as impious to question his merits
as those of an Apostle of Jesus. He is peculiarly appealed to as an advocate of the immortality of the
soul; and yet I will venture to say, that were there no
better arguments than his in proof of it, not a man
in the world would believe it. It is fortunate for us,

that Platonic republicanism has not obtained the same favor as Platonic Christianity; or we should now have been all living, men, women and children, pell mell together, like beasts of the field or forest. Yet "Plato is a great philosopher," said La Fontaine. But, says Fontenelle, "Do you find his ideas very clear?" "Oh no! he is of an obscurity impenetrable." "Do you not find him full of contradictions?" "Certainly," replied La Fontaine, "he is but a sophist." Yet immediately after he exclaims again, "Oh, Plato was a great philosopher." Socrates had reason, indeed, to complain of the misrepresentations of Plato; for in truth, his dialogues are libels on Socrates.

But why am I dosing you with these antediluvian topics? Because I am glad to have some one to whom they are familiar, and who will not receive them as if dropped from the moon. Our post-revolutionary youth are born under happier stars than you and I were. They acquire all learning in their mother's womb, and bring it into the world ready made. The information of books is no longer necessary; and all knowledge which is not innate, is in contempt, or neglect at least. Every folly must run its round; and so, I suppose, must that of self-learning and self-sufficiency; of rejecting the knowledge acquired in past ages, and starting on the new ground of intuition. When sobered by experience, I hope our successors will turn their attention to the advantages of education. I mean of education on the broad scale, and not that of the petty *academies,* as they call themselves, which are starting up in every neighborhood, and where one or two men, possessing Latin and sometimes Greek, a knowledge of the globes, and the first six books of Euclid, imagine and communicate this as the sum of science. They commit their pupils to the theatre of the world, with just taste enough of learning to be alienated from industrious pursuits, and not enough to do service in the ranks of science. We have some exceptions, indeed. I presented one to you lately, and we have some others. But the terms I use are general truths. I hope the necessity will, at length, be seen of establishing institutions here, as in Europe, where every branch of science, useful at this day, may be taught in its highest degree. Have you ever turned your thoughts to the plan of such an institution? I mean to a specification of the particular sciences of real use in human affairs, and how they might be so grouped as to require so many professors only as might bring them within the views of a just but enlightened economy? I should be happy in a communication of your ideas on this problem, either loose or digested. But to avoid my being run away with by another subject, and adding to the length and ennui of the present letter, I will here present to Mrs. Adams and yourself, the assurance of my constant and sincere friendship and respect.

TO GEORGE TICKNOR*

Poplar Forest near Lynchburg, Nov. 25. 1817.

DEAR SIR,—Your favor of Aug. 14. was delivered to me as I was setting out for the distant possession from which I now write, & to which I pay frequent & long visits. On my arrival here I make it my first duty to write the letter you request to Mr. Erving, and to inclose it in this under cover to your father that you may get it in time. My letters are always letters of thanks because you are always furnishing occasion for them. I am very glad you have been so kind as to make the alteration you mention in the Herodotus & Livy I had asked from the Messrs. Desbures. I have not yet heard from them, but daily expect to do so, and to learn the arrival of my books. I shall probably send them another catalogue early in spring; every supply from them furnishing additional materials for my happiness.

I had before heard of the military ingredients which Bonaparte had infused into all the schools of France, but have never so well understood them as from your

* Ford, 10:94–96.

letter. The penance he is now doing for all his atrocities must be soothing to every virtuous heart. It proves that we have a god in heaven. That he is just, and not careless of what passes in this world. And we cannot but wish to this inhuman wretch, a long, long life, that time as well as intensity may fill up his sufferings to the measure of his enormities. But indeed what sufferings can atone for his crimes against the liberties & happiness of the human race; for the miseries he has already inflicted on his own generation, & on those yet to come, on whom he has rivetted the chains of despotism!

I am now entirely absorbed in endeavours to effect the establishment of a general system of education in my native state, on the triple basis, 1, of elementary schools which shall give to the children of every citizen gratis, competent instruction in reading, writing, common arithmetic, and general geography. 2. Collegiate institutions for antient & modern languages, for higher instruction in arithmetic, geography & history, placing for these purposes a college within a day's ride of every inhabitant of the state, and adding a provision for the full education at the public expence of select subjects from among the children of the poor, who shall have exhibited at the elementary schools the most prominent indications of aptness of judgment & correct disposition. 3. An University in which all the branches of science deemed useful at this day, shall be taught in their highest degree. This would probably require ten or twelve professors, for most of whom we shall be obliged to apply to Europe, and most likely to Edinburg, because of the greater advantage the students will receive from communications made in their native language. This last establishment will probably be within a mile of Charlottesville, and four from Monticello, if the system should be adopted at all by our legislature who meet within a week from this time. My hopes however are kept in check by the ordinary character of our state legislatures, the members of which do not generally possess information enough to perceive the important truths, that knolege is power, that knolege is safety, and that knolege is happiness.

In the meantime, and in case of failure of the broader plan, we are establishing a college of general science, at the same situation near Charlottesville, the scale of which, of necessity will be much more moderate, as resting on private donations only. These amount at present to about 75,000 Dollars. The buildings are begun, and by midsummer we hope to have two or three professorships in operation. Would to god we could have two or three duplicates of yourself, the original being above our means and hopes. If then we fail in doing all the good we wish, we will do at least all we can. This is the law of duty in every society of free agents, where every one has equal right to judge for himself. God bless you, and give to the means of benefiting mankind which you will bring home with you, all the success your high qualifications ought to insure.

REPORT OF THE COMMISSIONERS APPOINTED TO FIX THE SITE OF THE UNIVERSITY OF VIRGINIA, &c.*

The Commissioners for the University of Virginia, having met, as by law required, at the tavern, in Rockfish Gap, on the Blue Ridge, on the first day of August, of this present year, 1818; and having formed a board, proceeded on that day to the discharge of the duties assigned to them by the act of the Legislature, entitled "An act, appropriating part of the revenue of the literary fund, and for other purposes;" and having continued their proceedings by adjournment, from day to day, to Tuesday, the 4th day of August, have agreed to a report on the several matters with which they were charged, which report they now respectfully address and submit to the Legislature of the State.

The first duty enjoined on them, was to enquire and

* Roy J. Honeywell, *The Educational Work of Thomas Jefferson* (Cambridge: Harvard University Press, 1931), pp. 248–60.

report a site, in some convenient and proper part of the State, for an university, to be called the "University of Virginia." In this enquiry, they supposed that the governing considerations should be the healthiness of the site, the fertility of the neighboring country, and its centrality to the white population of the whole State. For, although the act authorized and required them to receive any voluntary contributions, whether conditional or absolute, which might be offered through them to the President and Directors of the Literary Fund, for the benefit of the University, yet they did not consider this as establishing an auction, or as pledging the location to the highest bidder.

Three places were proposed, to wit: Lexington, in the county of Rockbridge, Staunton, in the county of Augusta, and the Central College, in the county of Albemarle. Each of these was unexceptionable as to healthiness and fertility. It was the degree of centrality to the white population of the State which alone then constituted the important point of comparison between these places; and the Board, after full enquiry, and impartial and mature consideration, are of opinion, that the central point of the white population of the State is nearer to the Central College than to either Lexington or Staunton, by great and important differences; and all other circumstances of the place in general being favorable to it, as a position for an university, they do report the Central College, in Albemarle, to be a convenient and proper part of the State for the University of Virginia.

2. The Board having thus agreed on a proper site for the University, to be reported to the Legislature, proceed to the second of the duties assigned to them— that of proposing a plan for its buildings—and they are of opinion that it should consist of distinct houses or pavilions, arranged at proper distances on each side of a lawn of a proper breadth, and of indefinite extent, in one direction, at least; in each of which should be a lecturing room, with from two to four apartments, for the accommodation of a professor and his family;

that these pavilions should be united by a range of dormitories, sufficient each for the accommodation of two students only, this provision being deemed advantageous to morals, to order, and to uninterrupted study; and that a passage of some kind, under cover from the weather, should give a communication along the whole range. It is supposed that such pavilions, on an average of the larger and smaller, will cost each about $5,000; each dormitory about $350, and hotels of a single room, for a refectory, and two rooms for the tenant, necessary for dieting the students, will cost about $3500 each. The number of these pavilions will depend on the number of professors, and that of the dormitories and hotels on the number of students to be lodged and dieted. The advantages of this plan are: greater security against fire and infection; tranquillity and comfort to the professors and their families thus insulated; retirement to the students: and the admission of enlargement to any degree to which the institution may extend in future times. It is suppposed probable, that a building of somewhat more size in the middle of the grounds may be called for in time, in which may be rooms for religious worship, under such impartial regulations as the Visitors shall prescribe, for public examinations, for a library, for the schools of music, drawing, and other associated purposes.

3, 4. In proceeding to the third and fourth duties prescribed by the Legislature, of reporting "the branches of learning, which should be taught in the University, and the number and description of the professorships they will require," the Commissioners were first to consider at what point it was understood that university education should commence? Certainly not with the alphabet, for reasons of expediency and impracticability, as well as from the obvious sense of the Legislature, who, in the same act, make other provision for the primary instruction of the poor children, expecting, doubtless, that in other cases it would be provided by the parent, or become, perhaps, subject of future and further attention of the Legislature. The objects of this primary education determine its character and limits. These objects would be,

To give to every citizen the information he needs for the transaction of his own business;

To enable him to calculate for himself, and to express and preserve his ideas, his contracts and accounts, in writing;

To improve, by reading, his morals and faculties;

To understand his duties to his neighbors and country, and to discharge with competence the functions confided to him by either;

To know his rights; to exercise with order and justice those he retains; to choose with discretion the fiduciary of those he delegates; and to notice their conduct with diligence, with candor, and judgment;

And, in general, to observe with intelligence and faithfulness all the social relations under which he shall be placed.

To instruct the mass of our citizens in these, their rights, interests and duties, as men and citizens, being then the objects of education in the primary schools, whether private or public, in them should be taught reading, writing and numerical arithmetic, the elements of mensuration (useful in so many callings,) and the outlines of geography and history. And this brings us to the point at which are to commence the higher branches of education, of which the Legislature require the development; those, for example, which are,

To form the statesmen, legislators and judges, on whom public prosperity and individual happiness are so much to depend;

To expound the principles and structure of government, the laws which regulate the intercourse of nations, those formed municipally for our own government, and a sound spirit of legislation, which, banishing all arbitrary and unnecessary restraint on individual action, shall leave us free to do whatever does not violate the equal rights of another;

To harmonize and promote the interests of agriculture, manufactures and commerce, and by well informed

views of political economy to give a free scope to the
public industry;

To develop the reasoning faculties of our youth, enlarge their minds, cultivate their morals, and instill into them the precepts of virtue and order;

To enlighten them with mathematical and physical
sciences, which advance the arts, and administer to the
health, the subsistence, and comforts of human life;

And, generally, to form them to habits of reflection
and correct action, rendering them examples of virtue
to others, and of happiness within themselves.

These are the objects of that higher grade of education, the benefits and blessings of which the Legislature now propose to provide for the good and ornament
of their country, the gratification and happiness of their
fellow-citizens, of the parent especially, and his progeny,
on which all his affections are concentrated.

In entering on this field, the Commissioners are aware
that they have to encounter much difference of opinion
as to the extent which it is expedient that this institution should occupy. Some good men, and even of respectable information, consider the learned sciences
as useless acquirements; some think that they do not
better the condition of man; and others that education,
like private and individual concerns, should be left to
private individual effort; not reflecting that an establishment embracing all the sciences which may be
useful and even necessary in the various vocations of
life, with the buildings and apparatus belonging to each,
are far beyond the reach of individual means, and must
either derive existence from public patronage, or not
exist at all. This would leave us, then, without those
callings which depend on education, or send us to other
countries to seek the instruction they require. But the
Commissioners are happy in considering the statute
under which they are assembled as proof that the Legislature is far from the abandonment of objects so interesting. They are sensible that the advantages of well-
directed education, moral, political and economical, are
truly above all estimate. Education generates habits of

application, of order, and the love of virtue; and controls, by the force of habit, any innate obliquities in our moral organization. We should be far, too, from the discouraging persuasion that man is fixed, by the law of his nature, at a given point; that his improvement is a chimera, and the hope delusive of rendering ourselves wiser, happier or better than our forefathers were. As well might it be urged that the wild and uncultivated tree, hitherto yielding sour and bitter fruit only, can never be made to yield better; yet we know that the grafting art implants a new tree on the savage stock, producing what is most estimable both in kind and degree. Education, in like manner, engrafts a new man on the native stock, and improves what in his nature was vicious and perverse into qualities of virtue and social worth. And it cannot be but that each generation succeeding to the knowledge acquired by all those who preceded it, adding to it their own acquisitions and discoveries, and handing the mass down for successive and constant accumulation, must advance the knowledge and well-being of mankind, not *infinitely*, as some have said, but *indefinitely*, and to a term which no one can fix and foresee. Indeed, we need look back half a century, to times which many now living remember well, and see the wonderful advances in the sciences and arts which have been made within that period. Some of these have rendered the elements themselves subservient to the purposes of man, have harnessed them to the yoke of his labors, and effected the great blessings of moderating his own, of accomplishing what was beyond his feeble force, and extending the comforts of life to a much enlarged circle, to those who had before known its necessaries only. That these are not the vain dreams of sanguine hope, we have before our eyes real and living examples. What, but education, has advanced us beyond the condition of our indigenous neighbors? And what chains them to their present state of barbarism and wretchedness, but a bigotted veneration for the supposed superlative wisdom of their fathers, and the preposterous idea that they are to look backward for better things, and not forward, longing, as it should seem, to return to the days of eating acorns and roots, rather than indulge in the degeneracies of civilization? And how much more encouraging to the achievements of science and improvement is this, than the desponding view that the condition of man cannot be ameliorated, that what has been must ever be, and that to secure ourselves where we are, we must tread with awful reverence in the footsteps of our fathers. This doctrine is the genuine fruit of the alliance between Church and State; the tenants of which, finding themselves but too well in their present condition, oppose all advances which might unmask their usurpations, and monopolies of honors, wealth, and power, and fear every change, as endangering the comforts they now hold. Nor must we omit to mention, among the benefits of education, the incalculable advantage of training up able counsellors to administer the affairs of our country in all its departments, legislative, executive and judiciary, and to bear their proper share in the councils of our national government; nothing more than education advancing the prosperity, the power, and the happiness of a nation.

Encouraged, therefore, by the sentiments of the Legislature, manifested in this statute, we present the following tabular statements of the branches of learning which we think should be taught in the University, forming them into groups, each of which are within the powers of a single professor:

> I. Languages, ancient:
>> Latin,
>> Greek,
>> Hebrew.
>
> II. Languages, modern:
>> French,
>> Spanish,
>> Italian,
>> German,
>> Anglo-Saxon.

III. Mathematics, pure:
        Algebra,
        Fluxions,
        Geometry, Elementary,
                Transcendal.
        Architecture, Military,
                Naval.

IV. Physico-Mathematics:
        Mechanics,
        Statics,
        Dynamics,
        Pneumatics,
        Acoustics,
        Optics,
        Astronomy,
        Geography.

V. Physics, or Natural Philosophy:
        Chemistry,
        Mineralogy.

VI. Botany,
        Zoölogy.

VII. Anatomy,
        Medicine.

VIII. Government,
        Political Economy,
        Law of Nature and Nations,
        History, being interwoven with Politics and Law.

IX. Law, municipal.

X. Ideology,
        General Grammar,
        Ethics,
        Rhetoric,
        Belles Lettres, and the fine arts.

Some of the terms used in this table being subject to a difference of acceptation, it is proper to define the meaning and comprehension intended to be given them here:

Geometry, Elementary, is that of straight lines and of
the circle.
Transcendental, is that of all other curves; it includes,
of course, *Projectiles,* a leading branch of the military
art.
Military Architecture includes Fortification, another
branch of that art.
Statics respect matter generally, in a state of rest, and
include Hydrostatics, or the laws of fluids particularly, at rest or in equilibrio.
Dynamics, used as a general term, include Dynamics
proper, or the laws of *solids* in motion; and Hydro-
dynamics, or Hydraulics, those of *fluids* in motion.
Pneumatics teach the theory of air, its weight, motion,
condensation, rarefaction, &c.
Acoustics, or Phonics, the theory of sound.
Optics, the laws of light and vision.
Physics, or Physiology, in a general sense, mean the doc-
trine of the physical objects of our senses.
Chemistry is meant, with its other usual branches, to
comprehend the theory of agriculture.
Mineralogy, in addition to its peculiar subjects, is here
understood to embrace what is real in geology.
Ideology is the doctrine of thought.
General Grammar explains the construction of language.

Some articles in this distribution of sciences will
need observation. A professor is proposed for ancient
languages, the Latin, Greek, and Hebrew, particularly;
but these languages being the foundation common to all
the sciences, it is difficult to foresee what may be the
extent of this school. At the same time, no greater obstruction to industrious study could be proposed than
the presence, the intrusions and the noisy turbulence
of a multitude of small boys; and if they are to be placed
here for the rudiments of the languages, they may be
so numerous that its character and value as an University
will be merged in those of a Grammar school. It is,
therefore, greatly to be wished, that preliminary schools,
either on private or public establishment, could be dis-

tributed in districts through the State, as preparatory to the entrance of students into the University. The tender age at which this part of education commences, generally about the tenth year, would weigh heavily with parents in sending their sons to a school so distant as the central establishment would be from most of them. Districts of such extent as that every parent should be within a day's journey of his son at school, would be desirable in cases of sickness, and convenient for supplying their ordinary wants, and might be made to lessen sensibly the expense of this part of their education. And where a sparse population would not, within such a compass, furnish subjects sufficient to maintain a school, a competent enlargement of district must, of necessity, there be submitted to. At these district schools or colleges, boys should be rendered able to read the easier authors, Latin and Greek. This would be useful and sufficient for many not intended for an University education. At these, too, might be taught English grammar, the higher branches of numerical arithmetic, the geometry of straight lines and of the circle, the elements of navigation, and geography to a sufficient degree, and thus afford to greater numbers the means of being qualified for the various vocations of life, needing more instruction than merely menial or praedial labor, and the same advantages to youths whose education may have been neglected until too late to lay a foundation in the learned languages. These institutions, intermediate between the primary schools and University, might then be the passage of entrance for youths into the University, where their classical learning might be critically completed, by a study of the authors of highest degree; and it is at this stage only that they should be received at the University. Giving then a portion of their time to a finished knowledge of the Latin and Greek, the rest might be appropriated to the modern languages, or to the commencement of the course of science for which they should be destined. This would generally be about the fifteenth year of their age, when they might go with more safety and contentment to that distance from their parents. Until this preparatory provision shall be made, either the University will be overwhelmed with the grammar school, or a separate establishment, under one or more ushers, for its lower classes, will be advisable, at a mile or two distant from the general one; where, too, may be exercised the stricter government necessary for young boys, but unsuitable for youths arrived at years of discretion.

The considerations which have governed the specification of languages to be taught by the professor of modern languages were, that the French is the language of general intercourse among nations, and as a depository of human science, is unsurpassed by any other language, living or dead; that the Spanish is highly interesting to us, as the language spoken by so great a portion of the inhabitants of our continents, with whom we shall probably have great intercourse ere long, and is that also in which is written the greater part of the earlier history of America. The Italian abounds with works of very superior order, valuable for their matter, and still more distinguished as models of the finest taste in style and composition. And the German now stands in a line with that of the most learned nations in richness of erudition and advance in the sciences. It is too of common descent with the language of our own country, a branch of the same original Gothic stock, and furnishes valuable illustrations for us. But in this point of view, the Anglo-Saxon is of peculiar value. We have placed it among the modern languages, because it is in fact that which we speak, in the earliest form in which we have knowledge of it. It has been undergoing, with time, those gradual changes which all languages, ancient and modern, have experienced; and even now needs only to be printed in the modern character and orthography to be intelligible, in a considerable degree, to an English reader. It has this value, too, above the Greek and Latin, that while it gives the radix of the mass of our language, they explain its innovations only. Obvious proofs of this have been presented to the modern reader in the disquisitions of Horn Tooke; and

Fortescue Aland has well explained the great instruction which may be derived from it to a full understanding of our ancient common law, on which, as a stock, our whole system of law is engrafted. It will form the first link in the chain of an historical review of our language through all its successive changes to the present day, will constitute the foundation of that critical instruction in it which ought to be found in a seminary of general learning, and thus reward amply the few weeks of attention which would alone be requisite for its attainment; a language already fraught with all the eminent science of our parent country, the future vehicle of whatever we may ourselves achieve, and destined to occupy so much space on the globe, claims distinguished attention in American education.

Medicine, where fully taught, is usually subdivided into several professorships, but this cannot well be without the accessory of an hospital, where the student can have the benefit of attending clinical lectures, and of assisting at operations of surgery. With this accessory, the seat of our University is not yet prepared, either by its population or by the numbers of poor who would leave their own houses, and accept of the charities of an hospital. For the present, therefore, we propose but a single professor for both medicine and anatomy. By him the medical science may be taught, with a history and explanations of all its successive theories from Hippocrates to the present day; and anatomy may be fully treated. Vegetable pharmacy will make a part of the botanical course, and mineral and chemical pharmacy of those of mineralogy and chemistry. This degree of medical information is such as the mass of scientific students would wish to possess, as enabling them in their course through life, to estimate with satisfaction the extent and limits of the aid to human life and health, which they may understandingly expect from that art; and it constitutes such a foundation for those intended for the profession, that the finishing course of practice at the bed-sides of the sick, and at the operations of surgery in a hospital, can neither be long nor expensive. To seek this finishing elsewhere, must therefore be submitted to for a while.

In conformity with the principles of our Constitution, which places all sects of religion on an equal footing, with the jealousies of the different sects in guarding that equality from encroachment and surprise, and with the sentiments of the Legislature in favor of freedom of religion, manifested on former occasions, we have proposed no professor of divinity; and the rather as the proofs of the being of a God, the creator, preserver, and supreme ruler of the universe, the author of all the relations of morality, and of the laws and obligations these infer, will be within the province of the professor of ethics; to which adding the developments of these moral obligations, of those in which all sects agree, with a knowledge of the languages, Hebrew, Greek, and Latin, a basis will be formed common to all sects. Proceeding thus far without offence to the Constitution, we have thought it proper at this point to leave every sect to provide, as they think fittest, the means of further instruction in their own peculiar tenets.

We are further of opinion, that after declaring by law that certain sciences shall be taught in the University, fixing the number of professors they require, which we think should, at present, be ten, limiting (except as to the professors who shall be first engaged in each branch,) a maximum for their salaries, (which should be a certain but moderate subsistence, to be made up by liberal tuition fees, as an excitement to assiduity), it will be best to leave to the discretion of the visitors, the grouping of these sciences together, according to the accidental qualifications of the professors; and the introduction also of other branches of science, when enabled by private donations, or by public provision, and called for by the increase of population, or other change of circumstances; to establish beginnings, in short, to be developed by time, as those who come after us shall find expedient. They will be more advanced than we are in science and in useful arts, and will know best what will suit the circumstances of their day.

We have proposed no formal provision for the gymnastics of the school, although a proper object of attention for every institution of youth. These exercises with ancient nations, constituted the principal part of the education of their youth. Their arms and mode of warfare rendered them severe in the extreme; ours, on the same correct principle, should be adapted to our arms and warfare; and the manual exercise, military manoeuvres, and tactics generally, should be the frequent exercise of the students, in their hours of recreation. It is at that age of aptness, docility, and emulation of the practices of manhood, that such things are soonest learnt and longest remembered. The use of tools too in the manual arts is worthy of encouragement, by facilitating to such as choose it, an admission into the neighboring workshops. To these should be added the arts which embellish life, dancing, music, and drawing; the last more especially, as an important part of military education. These innocent arts furnish amusement and happiness to those who, having time on their hands, might less inoffensively employ it. Needing, at the same time, no regular incorporation with the institution, they may be left to accessory teachers, who will be paid by the individuals employing them, the University only providing proper apartments for their exercise.

The fifth duty prescribed to the Commissioners, is to propose such general provisions as may be properly enacted by the Legislature, for the better organizing and governing the University.

In the education of youth, provision is to be made for, 1, tuition; 2, diet; 3, lodging; 4, government; and 5, honorary excitements. The first of these constitutes the proper functions of the professors; 2, the dieting of the students should be left to private boarding houses of their own choice, and at their own expense; to be regulated by the Visitors from time to time, the house only being provided by the University within its own precincts, and thereby of course subjected to the general regimen, moral or sumptuary, which they shall prescribe. 3. They should be lodged in dormitories, making a part of the general system of buildings. 4. The best mode of government for youth, in large collections, is certainly a desideratum not yet attained with us. It may be well questioned whether fear after a certain age, is a motive to which we should have ordinary recourse. The human character is susceptible of other incitements to correct conduct, more worthy of employ, and of better effect. Pride of character, laudable ambition, and moral dispositions are innate correctives of the indiscretions of that lively age; and when strengthened by habitual appeal and exercise, have a happier effect on future character than the degrading motive of fear. Hardening them to disgrace, to corporal punishments, and servile humiliations cannot be the best process for producing erect character. The affectionate deportment between father and son, offers in truth the best example for that of tutor and pupil; and the experience and practice of other countries, in this respect, may be worthy of enquiry and consideration with us. It will then be for the wisdom and discretion of the Visitors to devise and perfect a proper system of government, which, if it be founded in reason and comity, will be more likely to nourish in the minds of our youth the combined spirit of order and self-respect, so congenial with our political institutions, and so important to be woven into the American character. 5. What qualifications shall be required to entitle to entrance into the University, the arrangement of the days and hours of lecturing for the different schools, so as to facilitate to the students the circle of attendance on them; the establishment of periodical and public examinations, the premiums to be given for distinguished merit; whether honorary degrees shall be conferred, and by what appellations; whether the title to these shall depend on the time the candidate has been at the University, or, where nature has given a greater share of understanding, attention, and application; whether he shall not be allowed the advantages resulting from these endowments, with other minor items of government, we are of opinion should be entrusted to the Visitors; and the statute under which we act having provided for the appointment of these, we think they should moreover be charged with

The erection, preservation, and repair of the buildings, the care of the grounds and appurtenances, and of the interest of the University generally.

That they should have power to appoint a bursar, employ a proctor, and all other necessary agents.

To appoint and remove professors, two-thirds of the whole number of Visitors voting for the removal.

To prescribe their duties and the course of education, in conformity with the law.

To establish rules for the government and discipline of the students, not contrary to the laws of the land.

To regulate the tuition fees, and the rent of the dormitories they occupy.

To prescribe and control the duties and proceedings of all officers, servants, and others, with respect to the buildings, lands, appurtenances, and other property and interests of the University.

To draw from the literary fund such moneys as are by law charged on it for this institution; and in general

To direct and do all matters and things which, not being inconsistent with the laws of the land, to them shall seem most expedient for promoting the purposes of the said institution; which several functions they should be free to exercise in the form of by-laws, rules, resolutions, orders, instructions, or otherwise, as they should deem proper.

That they should have two stated meetings in the year, and occasional meetings at such times as they should appoint, or on a special call with such notice as themselves shall prescribe by a general rule; which meetings should be at the University, a majority of them constituting a quorum for business; and that on the death or resignation of a member, or on his removal by the President and Directors of the Literary Fund, or the Executive, or such other authority as the Legislature shall think best, such President and Directors, or the Executive, or other authority, shall appoint a successor.

That the said Visitors should appoint one of their own body to be Rector, and with him be a body corporate, under the style and title of the Rector and Visitors of the University of Virginia, with the right, as such, to use a common seal; that they should have capacity to plead and be impleaded in all courts of justice, and in all cases interesting to the University, which may be the subjects of legal cognizance and jurisdiction; which pleas should not abate by the determination of their office, but should stand revived in the name of their successors, and they should be capable in law and in trust for the University, of receiving subscriptions and donations, real and personal, as well from bodies corporate, or persons associated, as from private individuals.

And that the said Rector and Visitors should, at all times, conform to such laws as the Legislature may, from time to time, think proper to enact for their government; and the said University should, in all things, and at all times, be subject to the control of the Legislature.

And lastly, the Commissioners report to the Legislature the following conditional offers to the President and Directors of the Literary Fund, for the benefit of the University:

On the condition that Lexington, or its vicinity, shall be selected as the site of the University, and that the same be permanently established there within two years from the date, John Robinson, of Rockbridge county, has executed a deed to the President and Directors of the Literary Fund, to take effect at his death, for the following tracts of land, to wit:

400 acres on the North fork of James river, known by the name of Hart's bottom, purchased of the late Gen. Bowyer.

171 acres adjoining the same, purchased of James Griggsby.

203 acres joining the last mentioned tract, purchased of William Paxton.

112 acres lying on the North river, above the lands of Arthur Glasgow, conveyed to him by William Paxton's heirs.

500 acres adjoining the lands of Arthur Glasgow, Benjamin Camden and David Edmonson.

545 acres lying in Pryor's gap, conveyed to him by the heirs of William Paxton, deceased.

260 acres lying in Childer's gap, purchased of Wm. Mitchell.

300 acres lying, also, in Childer's gap, purchased of Nicholas Jones.

500 acres lying on Buffalo, joining the lands of Jas. Johnston.

340 acres on the Cowpasture river, conveyed to him by General James Breckenridge—reserving the right of selling the two last mentioned tracts, and converting them into other lands contiguous to Hart's bottom, for the benefit of the University; also, the whole of his slaves, amounting to 57 in number; one lot of 22 acres, joining the town of Lexington, to pass immediately on the establishment of the University, together with all the personal estate of every kind, subject only to the payment of his debts and fulfillment of his contracts.

It has not escaped the attention of the Commissioners, that the deed referred to is insufficient to pass the estate in the lands intended to be conveyed, and may be otherwise defective; but, if necessary, this defect may be remedied before the meeting of the Legislature, which the Commissioners are advised will be done.

The Board of Trustees of Washington College have also proposed to transfer the whole of their funds, viz: 100 shares in the funds of the James River Company, 31 acres of land upon which their buildings stand, their philosophical apparatus, their expected interest in the funds of the Cincinnati Society, the libraries of the Graham and Washington Societies, and $3,000 in cash, on condition that a reasonable provision be made for the present professors. A subscription has also been offered by the people of Lexington and its vicinity, amounting to $17,878, all which will appear from the deed and other documents, reference thereto being had.

In this case, also, it has not escaped the attention of the Commissioners, that questions may arise as to the power of the trustees to make the above transfers.

On the condition that the Central College shall be made the site of the University, its whole property, real and personal, in possession or in action, is offered. This consists of a parcel of land of 47 acres, whereon the buildings of the college are begun, one pavilion and its appendix of dormitories being already far advanced, and with one other pavilion, and equal annexation of dormitories, being expected to be completed during the present season—of another parcel of 153 acres, near the former, and including a considerable eminence very favorable for the erection of a future observatory; of the proceeds of the sales of two glebes, amounting to $3,280 86 cents; and of a subscription of $41,248, on papers in hand, besides what is on outstanding papers of unknown amount, not yet returned—out of these sums are to be taken, however, the cost of the lands, of the buildings, and other works done, and for existing contracts. For the conditional transfer of these to the President and Directors of the Literary Fund, a regular power, signed by the subscribers and founders of the Central College generally, has been given to its Visitors and Proctor, and a deed conveying the said property accordingly to the President and Directors of the Literary Fund, has been duly executed by the said Proctor, and acknowledged for record in the office of the clerk of the county court of Albemarle.

Signed and certified by the members present, each in his proper handwriting, this 4th day of August, 1818.

TH: JEFFERSON,	HUGH HOLMES,
CREED TAYLOR,	PHIL. C. PENDLETON,
PETER RANDOLPH,	SPENCER ROANE,
WM. BROCKENBROUGH,	JOHN M. C. TAYLOR,
ARCH'D RUTHERFORD,	J. G. JACKSON,

ARCH'D STUART,
JAMES BRECKENRIDGE,
HENRY E. WATKINS,
JAMES MADISON,
A. T. MASON,

PHIL. SLAUGHTER,
WM. H. CABELL,
NAT. H. CLAIBORNE,
WM. A. C. DADE,
WILLIAM JONES,

THOMAS WILSON.

TO JOSEPH C. CABELL*

Monticello, February 3, 1825.

DEAR SIR,—Although our Professors were, on the 5th of December, still in an English port, that they were safe raises me from the dead, for I was almost ready to give up the ship. That was eight weeks ago; they may therefore be daily expected.

In most public seminaries text-books are prescribed to each of the several schools, as the *norma docendi* in that school; and this is generally done by authority of the trustees. I should not propose this generally in our University, because I believe none of us are so much at the heights of science in the several branches, as to undertake this, and therefore that it will be better left to the Professors until occasion of interference shall be given. But there is one branch in which we are the best judges, in which heresies may be taught, of so interesting a character to our own State and to the United States, as to make it a duty in us to lay down the principles which are to be taught. It is that of government. Mr. Gilmer being withdrawn, we know not who his successor may be. He may be a Richmond lawyer, or one of that school of quondam federalism, now consolidation. It is our duty to guard against such principles being disseminated among our youth, and the diffusion of that poison, by a previous prescription of the texts to be followed in their discourses. I therefore enclose you a resolution which I think of

* Henry A. Washington, ed., *The Writings of Thomas Jefferson* (New York: Riker, Thorne, 1854), 7:397–99.

proposing at our next meeting, strictly confiding it to your own knowledge alone, and to that of Mr. Loyall, to whom you may communicate it, as I am sure it will harmonize with his principles. I wish it kept to ourselves, because I have always found that the less such things are spoken of beforehand, the less obstruction is contrived to be thrown in their way. I have communicated it to Mr. Madison.

Should the bill for district colleges pass in the end, our scheme of education will be complete. But the branch of primary schools may need attention, and should be brought, like the rest, to the forum of the legislature. The Governor, in his annual message, gives a favorable account of them in the lump. But this is not sufficient. We should know the operation of the law establishing these schools more in detail. We should know how much money is furnished to each county every year, and how much education it distributes every year, and such a statement should be laid before the legislature every year. The sum of education rendered in each county in each year should be estimated by adding together the number of months which each scholar attended, and stating the sum total of the months which all of them together attended, e. g., if in any county one scholar attended two months, three others four months each, eight others six months each, then the sum of these added together will make sixty-two months of schooling afforded in the county that year; and the number of sixty-two months entered in a table opposite to the name of the county, gives a satisfactory idea of the sum or quantum of education it rendered in that year. This will enable us to take many interesting and important views of the sufficiency of the plan established, and of the amendments necessary to produce the greatest effect. I enclose a form of the table which would be required, in which you will of course be sensible that the numbers entered are at hap-hazard, and *exempli gratia*, as I know nothing of the sums furnished or quantum of education rendered in each or any county. I send also the form of such a resolution as should be passed by the one or the other house, perhaps better in the lower one, and moved by some member nowise connected with us, for the less we appear before the house, the less we shall excite dissatisfaction.

I mentioned to you formerly our want of an anatomical hall for dissection. But if we get the fifty thousand dollars from Congress, we can charge to that, as the library fund, the six thousand dollars of the building fund which we have advanced for it in books and apparatus, and repaying from the former the six thousand dollars due to the latter, apply so much of it as is necessary for the anatomical building. No application on the subject need therefore be made to our legislature. But I hear nothing of our prospects before Congress. Yours affectionately.

Resolved, That the Governor be requested to have prepared and laid before the legislature, at their next session, a statement in detail of the sum of education which, under the law establishing primary schools, has been rendered in the schools of each county respectively: that it be stated in a tabular form, in the first column of which table shall be the names of the counties alphabetically arranged, and then, for every year, two other columns, in the first of which shall be entered, opposite to the name of each county, the sum of money furnished it in that year, and in the second shall be stated the sum of education rendered in the same county and year; which sum is to be estimated by adding together the number of months of schooling which the several individuals attending received. And that henceforward a similar statement be prepared and laid before the legislature every year for that year.

Accomac	. . .	$400	216 months schooling.
Albemarle	. . .	500	234	"
Amelia	. . .	250	183	"
Amherst	. . .	400	210	"
Augusta	. . .	800	461	"

&c.

MINUTES OF THE BOARD OF VISITORS OF
THE UNIVERSITY OF VIRGINIA*

March 4, 1825

. . . Whereas, it is the duty of this Board [of Visitors of the University of Virginia] to the government under which it lives, and especially to that of which this University is the immediate creation, to pay especial attention to the principles of government which shall be inculcated therein, and to provide that none shall be inculcated which are incompatible with those on which the Constitutions of this State, and of the United States were genuinely based, in the common opinion; and for this purpose it may be necessary to point out specially where these principles are to be found legitimately developed:

Resolved, that it is the opinion of this Board that as to the general principles of liberty and the rights of man, in nature and in society, the doctrines of Locke, in his "Essay concerning the true original extent and end of civil government," and of Sidney in his "Discourses on government," may be considered as those generally approved by our fellow citizens of this, and the United States, and that on the distinctive principles of the government of our State, and of that of the United States, the best guides are to be found in, 1. The Declaration of Independence, as the fundamental act of union of these States. 2. The book known by the title of "The Federalist," being an authority to which appeal is habitually made by all, and rarely declined or denied by any as evidence of the general opinion of those who framed, and of those who accepted the Constitution of the United States, on questions as to its genuine meaning. 3. The Resolutions of the General Assembly of Virginia in 1799 on the subject of the alien and sedition laws, which appeared to accord with the pre-

* Saul K. Padover, *The Complete Jefferson* (New York: Tudor, 1943), p. 1112.

dominant sense of the people of the United States. 4. The valedictory address of President Washington, as conveying political lessons of peculiar value. And that in the branch of the school of law, which is to treat on the subject of civil polity, these shall be used as the text and documents of the school. . . .

TO WILLIAM B. GILES*

Monticello, December 26, 1825.

. . . I learn with great satisfaction that your school is thriving well, and that you have at its head a truly classical scholar. He is one of three or four whom I can hear of in the State. We were obliged the last year to receive shameful Latinists into the classical school of the University, such as we will certainly refuse as soon as we can get from better schools a sufficiency of those properly instructed to form a class. We must get rid of this Connecticut Latin, of this barbarous confusion of long and short syllables, which renders doubtful whether we are listening to a reader of Cherokee, Shawnee, Iroquois, or what. Our University has been most fortunate in the five professors procured from England. A finer selection could not have been made. Besides their being of a grade of science which has left little superior behind, the correctness of their moral character, their accommodating dispositions, and zeal for the prosperity of the institution, leave us nothing more to wish. I verily believe that as high a degree of education can now be obtained here, as in the country they left. And a finer set of youths I never saw assembled for instruction. They committed some irregularities at first, until they learned the lawful length of their tether; since which it has never been transgressed in the smallest degree. A great proportion of them are severely devoted to study, and I fear not to say that within twelve or fifteen years from this time, a majority of the rulers of our State will have been educated here.

* Ford, 10:357.

They shall carry hence the correct principles of our day, and you may count assuredly that they will exhibit their country in a degree of sound respectability it has never known, either in our days, or those of our fore-fathers. I cannot live to see it. My joy must only be that of anticipation. But that you may see it in full fruition, is the probable consequence of the twenty years I am ahead of you in time, and is the sincere prayer of your affectionate and constant friend. . . .

5: Health, Learning, Virtue

> "Honesty is the first chapter in the book
> of wisdom."

*In nearly all of his discussions of education, whether
in public pronouncements or in private correspondence,
Jefferson showed himself thoroughly attuned to the
characteristic "new" outlook of the Enlightenment. His
pedagogy, like his political principles, was deeply imbued
with the naturalism or environmentalism of a Rousseau,
though he disavowed the extremes of Rousseau's ro-
manticism, and with the disciplinary concepts of a
Locke, though he tempered somewhat the crudities of
Locke's mechanistic psychology. More than either, however, Jefferson loved and honored the intellectual virtues and the intellectual life; but for him, as for them,
the chief ends of education were never held to be exclusively intellectual. Indeed, in certain respects, intellectual development was, for Jefferson, a chief means
to still higher ends: those of moral and civic excellence.
In the several letters contained in this section—letters
of advice to two young nephews (Thomas Mann Randolph and Peter Carr), to his fourteen-year-old daughter
(Martha Jefferson), and to his grandson (Thomas Jefferson
Randolph), as well as some observations to a dear friend
(Nathaniel Burwell) regarding the upbringing of his
daughter—Jefferson expounds on the theme of the
attitudes and the deportment that qualify one to live
the good life that he himself so handsomely exemplified.
From these, as indeed from his entire correspondence,
we see something of what Jefferson regarded as the
hallmarks, the attributes, of a truly educated—which is
to say, a truly free—man.*

SEE ALSO:

Letter to Martha Jefferson, April 7, 1787 (Boyd, 11: 277–78, or Koch-Peden, 419–20).

Letter to Thomas Mann Randolph, July 6, 1787 (Boyd, 11:556–59, or Koch-Peden, 424–26).

Letter to John Minor, August 30, 1814 (Ford, 9:480–85).

Letter to Thomas Jefferson Smith, February 21, 1825 (Ford, 10:340–41).

TO THOMAS MANN RANDOLPH, JR.*

DEAR SIR   Paris Aug. 27. 1786.

I am honoured with your favour of the 16th. instant, and desirous, without delay, of manifesting my wishes to be useful to you, I shall venture to you some thoughts on the course of your studies which must be submitted to the better advice with which your are surrounded. A longer race through life may have enabled me to seise some truths which have not yet been presented to your observation. A more intimate knowledge of the country in which you are to live and of the circumstances in which you will be placed, may enable me to point your attention to the branches of science which will administer the most to your happiness there. The foundations which you have laid in languages and mathematics are proper for every superstructure. The former exercises our memory while that and no other faculty is yet matured, and prevents our acquiring habits of idleness; the latter gives exercise to our reason, as soon as that has acquired a certain degree of strength, and stores the mind with truths which are useful in other branches of science. At this moment then a second order of preparation is to commence. I shall propose to you that it be extensive, comprehending Astronomy, Natural philosophy (or Physics) Natural history, Anatomy, Botany and Chemistry. No

* Julian P. Boyd, ed., *The Papers of Thomas Jefferson* (Princeton, N. J.: Princeton University Press, 1950 *et seq.*), 10:305–09.

inquisitive mind will be content to be ignorant of any
one of these branches. But I would advise you to be
contented with a course of lectures in most of them,
without attempting to make yourself completely master
of the whole. This is more than any genius, joined
to any length of life is equal to. You will find among
them some one study to which your mind will more
particularly attach itself. This then I would pursue
and propose to attain eminence in. Your own country
furnishes the most aliment for Natural history, Botany
and Physics, and as you express a fondness for the
former you might make it your principal object, endeavouring however to make myself more acquainted
with the two latter than with other branches likely to
be less useful. In fact you will find botany offering
it's charms to you at every step, during summer, and
Physics in every season. All these branches of science
will be better attained by attending courses of lectures
in them; you are now in a place where the best courses
upon earth are within your reach, and being delivered
in your native language, you lose no part of their benefit. Such an opportunity you will never again have. I
would therefore strongly press on you to fix no other
limitation to your stay in Edinburgh, than your having
got thro this whole circle. The omission of any one part
of it will be an affliction and a loss to you as long as
you live. Besides the comfort of knowlege, every science
is auxiliary to every other. While you are attending
these courses you can proceed by yourself in a regular
series of historical reading. It would be a waste of time
to attend a professor of this. It is to be acquired from
books, and if you pursue it by yourself, you can accomo-
date it to your other reading so as to fill up those
chasms of time not otherwise appropriated. There are
portions of the day too when the mind should be eased.
Particularly after dinner it should be applied to lighter
occupations. History is of this kind. It exercises principally the memory. Reflection also indeed is necessary,
but not generally in a laborious degree. To conduct
yourself in this branch of science you have only to con-

sider what aeras of it merit a general and what a
particular attention, and in each aera also to distinguish
between the countries the knowlege of whose history
will be useful, and those where it suffices only to be
not altogether ignorant. Having laid down your plan as
to the branches of history you would pursue, the order
of time will be your sufficient guide. After what you
have read in Antient history, I should suppose Millot's
digest would be useful and sufficient. The histories of
Greece and Rome are worthy a good degree of attention.
They should be read in the original authors. The transi-
tion from Antient to modern history will be best effected
by reading Gibbons, then a general history of the principal states of Europe, but particular ones of England.
Here too the original writers are to be preferred. Kennet
published a considerable collection of these in 3. vols.
folio but there are some others, not in his collection,
well worth being read. After the history of England,
that of America will claim your attention. Here too
original authors, and not compilers, are best. An author
who writes of his own times, or of times near his own,
presents in his own ideas and manner the best picture
of the moment of which he writes. History need not be
hurried, but may give way to the other sciences; because history can be pursued after you shall have left
your present situation, as well as while you remain in it.

When you shall have got thro' this second order
of preparation, the study of the law is to be begun.
This, like history, is to be acquired from books. All the
aid you will want will be a catalogue of the books to
be read, and the order in which they are to be read.
It being absolutely indifferent in what place you carry
on this reading, I should propose your doing it in
France. The advantages of this will be that you will
at the same time acquire the habit of speaking French
which is the object of a year or two, you may be giving
attention to such of the fine arts as your taste may
lead you to, and you will be forming an acquaintance
with the individuals and character of a nation with

whom we must long remain in the closest intimacy, and to whom we are bound by the strong ties of gratitude and policy; a nation in short of the most amiable dispositions on earth, the whole mass of which is penetrated with an affection for us. You might, before your return to your own country, make a visit to Italy also.

I should have performed the office of but half a friend were I to confine myself to the improvement of the mind only. Knowlege indeed is a desireable, a lovely possession, but I do not scruple to say that health is more so. It is of little consequence to store the mind with science if the body be permitted to become debilitated. If the body be feeble, the mind will not be strong. The sovereign invigorator of the body is exercise, and of all the exercises walking is best. A horse gives but a kind of half exercise, and a carriage is no better than a cradle. No one knows, till he tries, how easily a habit of walking is acquired. A person who never walked three miles will in the course of a month become able to walk 15. or 20. without fatigue. I have known some great walkers and had particular accounts of many more; and I never knew or heard of one who was not healthy and long lived. This species of exercise therefore is much to be advised. Should you be disposed to try it, as your health has been feeble, it will be necessary for you to begin with a little, and to increase it by degrees. For the same reason you must probably at first ascribe to it hours the most precious for study, I mean those about the middle of the day. But when you shall find yourself strong, you may venture to take your walks in the evening after the digestion of the dinner is pretty well over. This is making a composition between health and study. The latter would be too much interrupted were you to take from it the early hours of the day, and habit will soon render the evening's exercise as salutary as that of the morning. I speak this from my own experience, having, from an attachment to study, very early in life, made this arrangement of my time, having ever observed it, and still observing it, and always with perfect success.

Not less than two hours a day should be devoted to exercise, and the weather should be little regarded. A person not sick will not be injured by getting wet. It is but taking a cold bath, which never gives a cold to any one. Brute animals are the most healthy, and they are exposed to all weather, and of men, those are healthiest who are the most exposed. The recipe of those two descriptions of beings is simple diet, exercise and the open air, be it's state what it will; and we may venture to say that this recipe will give health and vigor to every other description.—By this time I am sure you will think I have sermonized enough. I have given you indeed a lengthy lecture. I have been led through it by my zeal to serve you; if in the whole you find one useful counsel, that will be my reward and a sufficient one. Few persons in your own country have started from as advantageous ground as that whereon you will be placed. Nature and fortune have been liberal to you. Every thing honourable or profitable there is placed within your own reach, and will depend on your own efforts. If these are exerted with assiduity, and guided by unswerving honesty, your success is infallible: and that it may be as great as you wish is the sincere desire of, Dear Sir, your most affectionate humble servant,   TH: JEFFERSON

P.S. Be so good as to present me affectionately to your brother and cousin.

TO PETER CARR, WITH ENCLOSURE*

DEAR PETER   Paris Aug. 10. 1787.

I have received your two letters of Decemb. 30. and April 18. and am very happy to find by them, as well as by letters from Mr. Wythe, that you have been so fortunate as to attract his notice and good will: I am sure you will find this to have been one of the most fortunate events of your life, as I have ever been sensible it was of mine. I inclose you a sketch of the sciences to which

* Boyd, 12:14–19.

I would wish you to apply in such order as Mr. Wythe shall advise: I mention also the books in them worth your reading, which submit to his correction. Many of these are among your father's books, which you should have brought to you. As I do not recollect those of them not in his library, you must write to me for them, making out a catalogue of such as you think you shall have occasion for in 18 months from the date of your letter, and consulting Mr. Wythe on the subject. To this sketch I will add a few particular observations.

1. Italian. I fear the learning this language will confound your French and Spanish. Being all of them degenerated dialects of the Latin, they are apt to mix in conversation. I have never seen a person speaking the three languages who did not mix them. It is a delightful language, but late events having rendered the Spanish more useful, lay it aside to prosecute that.

2. Spanish. Bestow great attention on this, and endeavor to acquire an accurate knowlege of it. Our future connections with Spain and Spanish America will render that language a valuable acquisition. The antient history of a great part of America too is written in that language. I send you a dictionary.

3. Moral philosophy. I think it lost time to attend lectures in this branch. He who made us would have been a pitiful bungler if he had made the rules of our moral conduct a matter of science. For one man of science, there are thousands who are not. What would have become of them? Man was destined for society. His morality therefore was to be formed to this object. He was endowed with a sense of right and wrong merely relative to this. This sense is as much a part of his nature as the sense of hearing, seeing, feeling; it is the true foundation of morality, and not the το χαλον truth, &c., as fanciful writers have imagined. The moral sense, or conscience, is as much a part of man as his leg or arm. It is given to all human beings in a stronger or weaker degree, as force of members is given them in a greater or less degree. It may be strengthened by exercise, as may any particular limb of the body. This sense is submitted

indeed in some degree to the guidance of reason: but it is a small stock which is required for this: even a less one than what we call Common sense. State a moral case to a ploughman and a professor. The former will decide it as well, and often better than the latter, because he has not been led astray by artificial rules. In this branch therefore read good books because they will encourage as well as direct your feelings. The writings of Sterne particularly form the best course of morality that ever was written. Besides these read the books mentioned in the inclosed paper; and above all things lose no occasion of exercising your dispositions to be grateful, to be generous, to be charitable, to be humane, to be true, just, firm, orderly, couragious &c. Consider every act of this kind as an exercise which will strengthen your moral faculties, and increase your worth.

4. Religion. Your reason is now mature enough to receive this object. In the first place divest yourself of all bias in favour of novelty and singularity of opinion. Indulge them in any other subject rather than that of religion. It is too important, and the consequences of error may be too serious. On the other hand shake off all the fears and servile prejudices under which weak minds are servilely crouched. Fix reason firmly in her seat, and call to her tribunal every fact, every opinion. Question with boldness even the existence of a god; because, if there be one, he must more approve the homage of reason, than that of blindfolded fear. You will naturally examine first the religion of your own country. Read the bible then, as you would read Livy or Tacitus. The facts which are within the ordinary course of nature you will believe on the authority of the writer, as you do those of the same kind in Livy and Tacitus. The testimony of the writer weighs in their favor in one scale, and their not being against the laws of nature does not weigh against them. But those facts in the bible which contradict the laws of nature, must be examined with more care, and under a variety of faces. Here you must recur to the pretensions of the writer to inspiration from

god. Examine upon what evidence his pretensions are
founded, and whether that evidence is so strong as that
it's falshood would be more improbable than a change of
the laws of nature in the case he relates. For example in
the book of Joshua we are told the sun stood still several
hours. Were we to read that fact in Livy or Tacitus we
should class it with their showers of blood, speaking of
statues, beasts &c., but it is said that the writer of that
book was inspired. Examine therefore candidly what evidence there is of his having been inspired. The preten-
sion is entitled to your enquiry, because millions believe
it. On the other hand you are Astronomer enough to
know how contrary it is to the law of nature that a body
revolving on it's axis, as the earth does, should have
stopped, should not by that sudden stoppage have pros-
trated animals, trees, buildings, and should after a certain time have resumed it's revolution, and that without
a second general prostration. Is this arrest of the earth's
motion, or the evidence which affirms it, most within the
law of probabilities? You will next read the new testament. It is the history of a personage called Jesus. Keep
in your eye the opposite pretensions. 1. Of those who
say he was begotten by god, born of a virgin, suspended
and reversed the laws of nature at will, and ascended
bodily into heaven: and 2. of those who say he was a
man, of illegitimate birth, of a benevolent heart, enthusiastic mind, who set out without pretensions to
divinity, ended in believing them, and was punished
capitally for sedition by being gibbeted according to the
Roman law which punished the first commission of that
offence by whipping, and the second by exile or death
in furcâ. See this law in the Digest Lib. 48. tit. 19 § 28. 3.
and Lipsius Lib. 2. de cruce. cap. 2. These questions are
examined in the books I have mentioned under the head
of religion, and several others. They will assist you in
your enquiries, but keep your reason firmly on the watch
in reading them all. Do not be frightened from this enquiry by any fear of it's consequences. If it ends in a
belief that there is no god, you will find incitements to

virtue in the comfort and pleasantness you feel in it's exercise, and the love of others which it will procure you. If you find reason to believe there is a god, a consciousness that you are acting under his eye, and that he approves you, will be a vast additional incitement. If that there be a future state, the hope of a happy existence in that increases the appetite to deserve it; if that Jesus was also a god, you will be comforted by a belief of his aid and love. In fine, I repeat that you must lay aside all prejudice on both sides, and neither believe nor reject any thing because any other person, or description of persons have rejected or believed it. Your own reason is the only oracle given you by heaven, and you are answerable not for the rightness but uprightness of the decision.—I forgot to observe when speaking of the New testament that you should read all the histories of Christ, as well of those whom a council of ecclesiastics have decided for us to be Pseudo-evangelists, as those they named Evangelists, because these Pseudo-evangelists pretended to inspiration as much as the others, and you are to judge their pretensions by your own reason, and not by the reason of those ecclesiastics. Most of these are lost. There are some however still extant, collected by Fabricius which I will endeavor to get and send you.

5. Travelling. This makes men wiser, but less happy. When men of sober age travel, they gather knowlege which they may apply usefully for their country, but they are subject ever after to recollections mixed with regret, their affections are weakened by being extended over more objects, and they learn new habits which cannot be gratified when they return home. Young men who travel are exposed to all these inconveniences in a higher degree, to others still more serious, and do not acquire that wisdom for which a previous foundation is requisite by repeated and just observations at home. The glare of pomp and pleasure is analogous to the motion of their blood, it absorbs all their affection and attention, they are torn from it as from the only good in this world, and return to their home as to a place of exile and condemnation. Their eyes are for ever turned back to the object

they have lost, and it's recollection poisons the residue of their lives. Their first and most delicate passions are hackneyed on unworthy objects here, and they carry home only the dregs, insufficient to make themselves or any body else happy. Add to this that a habit of idleness, an inability to apply themselves to business is acquired and renders them useless to themselves and their country. These observations are founded in experience. There is no place where your pursuit of knowlege will be so little obstructed by foreign objects as in your own country, nor any wherein the virtues of the heart will be less exposed to be weakened. Be good, be learned, and be industrious, and you will not want the aid of travelling to render you precious to your country, dear to your friends, happy within yourself. I repeat my advice to take a great deal of exercise, and on foot. Health is the first requisite after morality. Write to me often and be assured of the interest I take in your success, as well as of the warmth of those sentiments of attachment with which I am, dear Peter, your affectionate friend,

TH: JEFFERSON

P.S. Let me know your age in your next letter. Your cousins here are well and desire to be remembered to you.

ENCLOSURE

Antient history. Herodot. Thucyd. Xenoph. hellen. Xenoph. Anab. Q. Curt. Just.
　Livy. Polybius. Sallust. Caesar. Suetonius. Tacitus. Aurel. Victor. Herodian.
　Gibbons' decline of the Roman empire. Milot histoire ancienne.
Mod. hist. English. Tacit. Germ. & Agricole. Hume to the end of H.VI. then Habington's E.IV.—Sr. Thomas Moor's E.5. & R.3.—Ld. Bacon's H.7.—Ld. Herbert of Cherbury's H.8.—K. Edward's journal (in Burnet) Bp. of Hereford's E.6. & Mary.—Cambden's Eliz. Wilson's Jac.I. Ludlow (omit Clarendon as too seducing for a young republican. By and by read him) Burnet's

Charles 2. Jac.2. Wm. & Mary & Anne.—Ld. Orrery
down to George 1. & 2.—Burke's G.3. Robertson's hist.
of Scotland.

American. Robertson's America.—Douglass's N. America.
—Hutcheson's Massachusets, Smith's N. York.—Smith's
N. Jersey.—Franklin's review of Pennsylvania. Smith's,
Stith's, Keith's, & Beverley's hist. of Virginia.

Foreign. Mallet's Northn. Antiquities by Percy.—Puffen-
dorf's histy. of Europe & Martiniere's of Asia, Africa &
America.—Milot histoire Moderne. Voltaire histoire
universelle.—Milot hist. de France.—Mariana's hist. of
Spain in Spa[nish.]—Robertson's Charles V.—Watson's
Phil. II. & III.—Grotii Belgica.
Mosheim's Ecclesiastical history.

Poetry. Homer—Milton—Ossian—Sophocles—Aeschylus
—Eurip.—Metastasio—Shakesp.—Theocritus—Anac-
reon [. . .]

Mathematics. Bezout & whatever else Mr. Madison rec-
ommends.

Astronomy. Delalande &c. as Mr. Madison shall recommend.

Natural Philosophy. Musschenbroeck.

Botany. Linnaei Philosophia Botanica—Genera Plantarum—Species plantarum—Gronovii flora [Virginica.]

Chemistry. Fourcroy.

Agriculture. Home's principles of Agriculture—Tull &c.

Anatomy. Cheselden.

Morality. The Socratic dialogues—Cicero's Philosophies
—Kaim's principles of Natl. religion—Helvetius de
l'esprit et de l'homme. Locke's Essay.—Lucretius—
Traité de Morale & du Bon[heur]

Religion. Locke's Conduct of the mind.—Middleton's
works—Bolingbroke's philosoph. works—Hume's es-
says—Voltaire's works—Beattie.

Politics & Law. Whatever Mr. Wythe pleases, who will be
so good as to correct also all the preceding articles
which are only intended as a ground work to be
finished by his pencil.

TO MARTHA JEFFERSON*

Aix en Provence March. 28. 1787.

I was happy, my dear Patsy, to receive, on my arrival here, your letter informing me of your health and occupations. I have not written to you sooner because I have been almost constantly on the road. My journey hitherto has been a very pleasing one. It was undertaken with the hope that the mineral waters of this place might restore strength to my wrist. Other considerations also concurred. Instruction, amusement, and abstraction from business, of which I had too much at Paris. I am glad to learn that you are employed in things new and good in your music and drawing. You know what have been my fears for some time past; that you do not employ yourself so closely as I could wish. You have promised me a more assiduous attention, and I have great confidence in what you promise. It is your future happiness which interests me, and nothing can contribute more to it (moral rectitude always excepted) than the contracting a habit of industry and activity. Of all the cankers of human happiness, none corrodes it with so silent, yet so baneful a tooth, as indolence. Body and mind both unemployed, our being becomes a burthen, and every object about us loathsome, even the dearest. Idleness begets ennui, ennui the hypochrondria, and that a diseased body. No laborious person was ever yet hysterical. Exercise and application produce order in our affairs, health of body, chearfulness of mind, and these make us precious to our friends. It is while we are young that the habit of industry is formed. If not then, it never is afterwards. The fortune of our lives therefore depends on employing well the short period of youth. If at any moment, my dear, you catch yourself in idleness, start from it as you would from the precipice of a gulph. You are not however to consider yourself as unemployed while taking exercise. That is necessary for your health, and health is the first

* Boyd, 11:250–52.

of all objects. For this reason if you leave your dancing master for the summer, you must increase your other exercise. I do not like your saying that you are unable to read the antient print of your Livy, but with the aid of your master. We are always equal to what we undertake with resolution. A little degree of this will enable you to decypher your Livy. If you always lean on your master, you will never be able to proceed without him. It is a part of the American character to consider nothing as desperate; to surmount every difficulty by resolution and contrivance. In Europe there are shops for every want. It's inhabitants therefore have no idea that their wants can be furnished otherwise. Remote from all other aid, we are obliged to invent and to execute; to find means within ourselves, and not to lean on others. Consider therefore the conquering your Livy as an exercise in the habit of surmounting difficulties, a habit which will be necessary to you in the country where you are to live, and without which you will be thought a very helpless animal, and less esteemed. Music, drawing, books, invention and exercise will be so many resources to you against ennui. But there are others which to this object add that of utility. These are the needle, and domestic oeconomy. The latter you cannot learn here, but the former you may. In the country life of America there are many moments when a woman can have recourse to nothing but her needle for employment. In a dull company and in dull weather for instance. It is ill manners to read; it is ill manners to leave them; no cardplaying there among genteel people; that is abandoned to blackguards. The needle is then a valuable resource. Besides without knowing to use it herself, how can the mistress of a family direct the works of her servants? You ask me to write you long letters. I will do it my dear, on condition you will read them from time to time, and practice what they will inculcate. Their precepts will be dictated by experience, by a perfect knowlege of the situation in which you will be placed, and by the fondest love for you. This it is which makes me wish to see you more qualified than common. My expectations from you are high: yet not

higher than you may attain. Industry and resolution are
all that are wanting. No body in this world can make me
so happy, or so miserable as you. Retirement from public
life will ere long become necessary for me. To your sister
and yourself I look to render the evening of my life
serene and contented. It's morning has been clouded by
loss after loss till I have nothing left but you. I do not
doubt either your affection or dispositions. But great
exertions are necessary, and you have little time left to
make them. Be industrious then, my dear child. Think
nothing unsurmountable by resolution and application,
and you will be all that I wish you to be. You ask me if
it is my desire you should dine at the abbess's table? It is.
Propose it as such to Madame de Traubenheim with my
respectful compliments and thanks for her care of you.
Continue to love me with all the warmth with which you
are beloved by, my dear Patsy, yours affectionately,

TH: JEFFERSON

TO NATHANIEL BURWELL*

Monticello, March 14, 1818.

DEAR SIR,—Your letter of February 17th found me
suffering under an attack of rheumatism, which has but
now left me at sufficient ease to attend to the letters I
have received. A plan of female education has never been
a subject of systematic contemplation with me. It has
occupied my attention so far only as the education of my
own daughters occasionally required. Considering that
they would be placed in a country situation, where little
aid could be obtained from abroad, I thought it essential
to give them a solid education, which might enable them,
when become mothers, to educate their own daughters,
and even to direct the course for sons, should their fathers be lost, or incapable, or inattentive. My surviving
daughter accordingly, the mother of many daughters as
well as sons, has made their education the object of her

* Paul L. Ford, ed., *The Writings of Thomas Jefferson* (New
York: G. P. Putnam's Sons, 1892–1899), 10:104–06.

life, and being a better judge of the practical part than myself, it is with her aid and that of one of her élèves that I shall subjoin a catalogue of the books for such a course of reading as we have practiced.

A great obstacle to good education is the inordinate passion prevalent for novels, and the time lost in that reading which should be instructively employed. When this poison infects the mind, it destroys its tone and revolts it against wholesome reading. Reason and fact, plain and unadorned, are rejected. Nothing can engage attention unless dressed in all the figments of fancy, and nothing so bedecked comes amiss. The result is a bloated imagination, sickly judgment, and disgust towards all the real businesses of life. This mass of trash, however, is not without some distinction; some few modelling their narratives, although fictitious, on the incidents of real life, have been able to make them interesting and useful vehicles of a sound morality. Such, I think, are Marmontel's new moral tales, but not his old ones, which are really immoral. Such are the writings of Miss Edgeworth, and some of those of Madame Genlis. For a like reason, too, much poetry should not be indulged. Some is useful for forming style and taste. Pope, Dryden, Thompson, Shakspeare, and of the French, Molière, Racine, the Corneilles, may be read with pleasure and improvement.

The French language, become that of the general intercourse of nations, and from their extraordinary advances, now the depository of all science, is an indispensable part of education for both sexes. In the subjoined catalogue, therefore, I have placed the books of both languages indifferently, according as the one or the other offers what is best.

The ornaments too, and the amusements of life, are entitled to their portion of attention. These, for a female, are dancing, drawing, and music. The first is a healthy exercise, elegant and very attractive for young people. Every affectionate parent would be pleased to see his daughter qualified to participate with her companions, and without awkwardness at least, in the circles of festivity, of which she occasionally becomes a part. It is a necessary accomplishment, therefore, although of short use, for the French rule is wise, that no lady dances after marriage. This is founded in solid physical reasons, gestation and nursing leaving little time to a married lady when this exercise can be either safe or innocent. Drawing is thought less of in this country than in Europe. It is an innocent and engaging amusement, often useful, and a qualification not to be neglected in one who is to become a mother and an instructor. Music is invaluable where a person has an ear. Where they have not, it should not be attempted. It furnishes a delightful recreation for the hours of respite from the cares of the day, and lasts us through life. The taste of this country, too, calls for this accomplishment more strongly than for either of the others.

I need say nothing of household economy, in which the mothers of our country are generally skilled, and generally careful to instruct their daughters. We all know its value, and that diligence and dexterity in all its processes are inestimable treasures. The order and economy of a house are as honorable to the mistress as those of the farm to the master, and if either be neglected, ruin follows, and children destitute of the means of living.

This, Sir, is offered as a summary sketch on a subject on which I have not thought much. It probably contains nothing but what has already occurred to yourself, and claims your acceptance on no other ground than as a testimony of my respect for your wishes, and of my great esteem and respect.

TO THOMAS JEFFERSON RANDOLPH *

Washington November 24, 1808.

MY DEAR JEFFERSON,—I have just received the enclosed letter under cover from Mr. Bankhead which I presume is from Anne, and will inform you she is well. Mr. Bankhead has consented to go & pursue his studies at Monti-

* Ford, 9:230–34.

cello, and live with us till his pursuits or circumstances may require a separate establishment. Your situation, thrown at such a distance from us, & alone, cannot but give us all great anxieties for you. As much has been secured for you, by your particular position and the acquaintance to which you have been recommended, as could be done towards shielding you from the dangers which surround you. But thrown on a wide world, among entire strangers, without a friend or guardian to advise, so young too and with so little experience of mankind, your dangers are great, & still your safety must rest on yourself. A determination never to do what is wrong, prudence and good humor, will go far towards securing to you the estimation of the world. When I recollect that at 14 years of age, the whole care & direction of myself was thrown on myself entirely, without a relation or friend qualified to advise or guide me, and recollect the various sorts of bad company with which I associated from time to time, I am astonished I did not turn off with some of them, & become as worthless to society as they were. I had the good fortune to become acquainted very early with some characters of very high standing, and to feel the incessant wish that I could ever become what they were. Under temptations & difficulties, I would ask myself what would Dr. Small, Mr. Wythe, Peyton Randolph do in this situation? What course in it will insure me their approbation? I am certain that this mode of deciding on my conduct, tended more to its correctness than any reasoning powers I possessed. Knowing the even & dignified line they pursued, I could never doubt for a moment which of two courses would be in character for them. Whereas, seeking the same object through a process of moral reasoning, & with the jaundiced eye of youth, I should often have erred. From the circumstances of my position, I was often thrown into the society of horse racers, card players, fox hunters, scientific & professional men, and of dignified men; and many a time have I asked myself, in the enthusiastic moment of the death of a fox, the victory of a favorite horse, the issue of a question eloquently argued at the bar, or in

the great council of the nation, well, which of these kinds
of reputation should I prefer? That of a horse jockey?
a fox hunter? an orator? or the honest advocate of my
country's rights? Be assured, my dear Jefferson, that these
little returns into ourselves, this self-catechising habit, is
not trifling nor useless, but leads to the prudent selection
& steady pursuit of what is right.

I have mentioned good humor as one of the preserva-
tives of our peace & tranquillity. It is among the most
effectual, and its effect is so well imitated and aided,
artificially, by politeness, that this also becomes an acquisition of first rate value. In truth, politeness is artificial
good humor, it covers the natural want of it, & ends by
rendering habitual a substitute nearly equivalent to the
real virtue. It is the practice of sacrificing to those whom
we meet in society, all the little conveniences & prefer-
ences which will gratify them, & deprive us of nothing
worth a moment's consideration; it is the giving a pleasing & flattering turn to our expressions, which will conciliate others, and make them pleased with us as well as
themselves. How cheap a price for the good will of another! When this is in return for a rude thing said by
another, it brings him to his senses, it mortifies & cor-
rects him in the most salutary way, and places him at the
feet of your good nature, in the eyes of the company. But
in stating prudential rules for our government in society,
I must not omit the important one of never entering into
dispute or argument with another. I never saw an instance of one of two disputants convincing the other by
argument. I have seen many, on their getting warm, be-
coming rude, & shooting one another. Conviction is the
effect of our own dispassionate reasoning, either in soli-
tude, or weighing within ourselves, dispassionately, what
we hear from others, standing uncommitted in argument
ourselves. It was one of the rules which, above all others,
made Doctor Franklin the most amiable of men in society, "never to contradict anybody." If he was urged to
announce an opinion, he did it rather by asking questions, as if for information, or by suggesting doubts.
When I hear another express an opinion which is not

mine, I say to myself, he has a right to his opinion, as I
to mine; why should I question it? His error does me no
injury, and shall I become a Don Quixote, to bring all
men by force of argument to one opinion? If a fact be
misstated, it is probable he is gratified by a belief of it, &
I have no right to deprive him of the gratification. If
he wants information, he will ask it, & then I will give it
in measured terms; but if he still believes his own story,
& shows a desire to dispute the fact with me, I hear him
& say nothing. It is his affair, not mine, if he prefers
error. There are two classes of disputants most frequently
to be met with among us. The first is of young students,
just entered the threshold of science, with a first view of
its outlines, not yet filled up with the details & modifica-
tions which a further progress would bring to their
knoledge. The other consists of the ill-tempered & rude
men in society, who have taken up a passion for politics.
(Good humor & politeness never introduce into mixed
society, a question on which they foresee there will be a
difference of opinion.) From both of those classes of disputants, my dear Jefferson, keep aloof, as you would
from the infected subjects of yellow fever or pestilence.
Consider yourself, when with them, as among the pa-
tients of Bedlam, needing medical more than moral
counsel. Be a listener only, keep within yourself, and
endeavor to establish with yourself the habit of silence,
especially on politics. In the fevered state of our country,
no good can ever result from any attempt to set one of
these fiery zealots to rights, either in fact or principle.
They are determined as to the facts they will believe,
and the opinions on which they will act. Get by them,
therefore, as you would by an angry bull; it is not for a
man of sense to dispute the road with such an animal.
You will be more exposed than others to have these animals shaking their horns at you, because of the relation
in which you stand with me. Full of political venom, and
willing to see me & to hate me as a chief in the antagonist
party, your presence will be to them what the vomit
grass is to the sick dog, a nostrum for producing ejacula-
tion. Look upon them exactly with that eye, and pity

them as objects to whom you can administer only occasional ease. My character is not within their power. It is in the hands of my fellow citizens at large, and will be consigned to honor or infamy by the verdict of the republican mass of our country, according to what themselves will have seen, not what their enemies and mine shall have said. Never, therefore, consider these puppies in politics as requiring any notice from you, & always show that you are not afraid to leave my character to the umpirage of public opinion. Look steadily to the pursuits which have carried you to Philadelphia, be very select in the society you attach yourself to, avoid taverns, drinkers, smokers, idlers, & dissipated persons generally; for it is with such that broils & contentions arise; and you will find your path more easy and tranquil. The limits of my paper warn me that it is time for me to close with my affectionate adieu.

P. S. Present me affectionately to Mr. Ogilvie, &, in doing the same to Mr. Peale, tell him I am writing with his polygraph, & shall send him mine the first moment I have leisure enough to pack it.

Epilogue

> "... knowledge is power ... ignorance
> is weakness."

*The most famous, and in some respects the most signifi-
cant, conversation in American history was that carried
on in the extended correspondence between Thomas Jefferson and John Adams. Staunch colleagues during the
revolutionary period and immediately thereafter, these
two became bitter political opponents, scarcely speaking
to each other for the decade following Jefferson's election
to the presidency. The relationship was resumed in all
its intimacy in 1812—and for the rest of their lives (both
of them died on the same fateful day: July 4, 1826) they
were in constant communication. Their discussions
ranged over all manner of topics, but most often they
dwelt upon matters philosophical and political. Placing
education squarely within such a context, the letter which
follows provides a fitting conclusion to this volume for,
as Jefferson there remarks, the advancement of popular
intelligence constitutes "the keystone of the arch of our
government."*

TO JOHN ADAMS*

Monticello October 28, 1813.

DEAR SIR,—According to the reservation between us,
of taking up one of the subjects of our correspondence
at a time, I turn to your letters of August the 16th and
September the 2d.

* Paul L. Ford, ed., *The Writings of Thomas Jefferson* (New
York: G. P. Putnam's Sons, 1892–1899), 9:424–30.

The passage you quote from Theognis, I think has an
ethical rather than a political object. The whole piece
is a moral *exhortation*, παραινεσις, and this passage particularly seems to be a reproof to man, who while with
his domestic animals he is curious to improve the race,
by employing always the finest male, pays no attention
to the improvement of his own race, but intermarries
with the vicious, the ugly, or the old, for considerations
of wealth or ambition. It is in conformity with the principle adopted afterwards by the Pythagoreans, and expressed by Ocellus in another form; περι δε τῆς ἐκ τῶν
αλληλων ανθρωπων γενεσεως &c.—ουχ ηδονης ενεκα η μιξις:
which, as literally as intelligibility will admit, may be
thus translated: "concerning the inter-procreation of
men, how, and of whom it shall be, in a perfect manner,
and according to the laws of modesty and sanctity, con-
jointly, this is what I think right. First to lay it down
that we do not commix for the sake of pleasure, but of
the procreation of children. For the powers, the organs
and desires for coition have not been given by God to
man for the sake of pleasure, but for the procreation of
the race. For as it were incongruous, for a mortal born
to partake of divine life, the immortality of the race
being taken away, God fulfilled the purpose by making
the generations uninterrupted and continuous. This,
therefore, we are especially to lay down as a principle,
that coition is not for the sake of pleasure." But nature,
not trusting to this moral and abstract motive, seems to
have provided more securely for the perpetuation of the
species, by making it the effect of the *oestrum* implanted
in the constitution of both sexes. And not only has the
commerce of love been indulged on this unhallowed im-
pulse, but made subservient also to wealth and ambition
by marriage, without regard to the beauty, the healthiness, the understanding, or virtue of the subject from
which we are to breed. The selecting the best male for a
Harem of well chosen females also, which Theognis
seems to recommend from the example of our sheep and
asses, would doubtless improve the human, as it does the
brute animal, and produce a race of veritable αριστοι.

For experience proves, that the moral and physical qualities of man, whether good or evil, are transmissible in a
certain degree from father to son. But I suspect that the
equal rights of men will rise up against this privileged
Solomon and his Harem, and oblige us to continue acquiescence under the "Αμαυρωσις γενεος αστων" which
Theognis complains of, and to content ourselves with
the accidental aristoi produced by the fortuitous con-
course of breeders. For I agree with you that there is a
natural aristocracy among men. The grounds of this are
virtue and talents. Formerly, bodily powers gave place
among the aristoi. But since the invention of gunpowder
has armed the weak as well as the strong with missile
death, bodily strength, like beauty, good humor, politeness and other accomplishments, has become but an
auxiliary ground for distinction. There is also an artificial aristocracy, founded on wealth and birth, without
either virtue or talents; for with these it would belong to
the first class. The natural aristocracy I consider as the
most precious gift of nature, for the instruction, the
trusts, and government of society. And indeed, it would
have been inconsistent in creation to have formed man
for the social state, and not to have provided virtue and
wisdom enough to manage the concerns of the society.
May we not even say, that that form of government is
the best, which provides the most effectually for a pure
selection of these natural aristoi into the offices of government? The artificial aristocracy is a mischievous ingredient in government, and provision should be made
to prevent its ascendency. On the question, what is the
best provision, you and I differ; but we differ as rational
friends, using the free exercise of our own reason, and
mutually indulging its errors. You think it best to put
the pseudo-aristoi into a separate chamber of legislation,
where they may be hindered from doing mischief by
their co-ordinate branches, and where, also, they may
be a protection to wealth against the Agrarian and
plundering enterprises of the majority of the people. I
think that to give them power in order to prevent them
from doing mischief, is arming them for it, and increas-

ing instead of remedying the evil. For if the co-ordinate branches can arrest their action, so may they that of the co-ordinates. Mischief may be done negatively as well as positively. Of this, a cabal in the Senate of the United States has furnished many proofs. Nor do I believe them necessary to protect the wealthy; because enough of these will find their way into every branch of the legislation, to protect themselves. From fifteen to twenty legislatures of our own, in action for thirty years past, have proved that no fears of an equalization of property are to be apprehended from them. I think the best remedy is exactly that provided by all our constitutions, to leave to the citizens the free election and separation of the aristoi from the pseudo-aristoi, of the wheat from the chaff. In general they will elect the really good and wise. In some instances, wealth may corrupt, and birth blind them; but not in sufficient degree to endanger the society.

It is probable that our difference of opinion may, in some measure, be produced by a difference of character in those among whom we live. From what I have seen of Massachusetts and Connecticut myself, and still more from what I have heard, and the character given of the former by yourself, who know them so much better, there seems to be in those two States a traditionary reverence for certain families, which has rendered the offices of the government nearly hereditary in those families. I presume that from an early period of your history, members of those families happening to possess virtue and talents, have honestly exercised them for the good of the people, and by their services have endeared their names to them. In coupling Connecticut with you, I mean it politically only, not morally. For having made the Bible the common law of their land, they seemed to have modeled their morality on the story of Jacob and Laban. But although this hereditary succession to office with you, may, in some degree, be founded in real family merit, yet in a much higher degree, it has proceeded from your strict alliance of Church and State. These families are canonised in the eyes of the people on common principles, "you tickle me, and I will tickle you." In Virginia we have nothing of this. Our clergy, before the revolution, having been secured against rivalship by fixed salaries, did not give themselves the trouble of acquiring influence over the people. Of wealth, there were great accumulations in particular families, handed down from generation to generation, under the English law of entails. But the only object of ambition for the wealthy was a seat in the King's Council. All their court then was paid to the crown and its creatures; and they Philipised in all collisions between the King and the people. Hence they were unpopular; and that unpopularity continues attached to their names. A Randolph, a Carter, or a Burwell must have great personal superiority over a common competitor to be elected by the people even at this day. At the first session of our legislature after the Declaration of Independence, we passed a law abolishing entails. And this was followed by one abolishing the privilege of primogeniture, and dividing the lands of intestates equally among all their children, or other representatives. These laws, drawn by myself, laid the ax to the foot of pseudo-aristocracy. And had another which I prepared been adopted by the legislature, our work would have been complete. It was a bill for the more general diffusion of learning. This proposed to divide every county into wards of five or six miles square, like your townships; to establish in each ward a free school for reading, writing and common arithmetic; to provide for the annual selection of the best subjects from these schools, who might receive, at the public expense, a higher degree of education at a district school; and from these district schools to select a certain number of the most promising subjects, to be completed at an University, where all the useful sciences should be taught. Worth and genius would thus have been sought out from every condition of life, and completely prepared by education for defeating the competition of wealth and birth for public trusts. My proposition had, for a further object, to impart to these wards those portions of self-government for which they are best qualified, by confiding to them the care of their poor, their roads, police, elections, the nomination of jurors, administration of justice in small cases, elementary exercises of militia; in short, to have made them little republics, with a warden at the head of each, for all those concerns which, being under their eye, they would better manage than the larger republics of the county or State. A general call of ward meetings by their wardens on the same day through the State, would at any time produce the genuine sense of the people on any required point, and would enable the State to act in mass, as your people have so often done, and with so much effect by their town meetings. The law for religious freedom, which made a part of this system, having put down the aristocracy of the clergy, and restored to the citizen the freedom of the mind, and those of entails and descents nurturing an equality of condition among them, this on education would have raised the mass of the people to the high ground of moral respectability necessary to their own safety, and to orderly government; and would have completed the great object of qualifying them to select the veritable aristoi, for the trusts of government, to the exclusion of the pseudalists; and the same Theognis who has furnished the epigraphs of your two letters, assures us that "Ουδεμιαν πω, Κυρν,' αγαθοι πολιν ωλεσαν ανδρες." Although this law has not yet been acted on but in a small and inefficient degree, it is still considered as before the legislature, with other bills of the revised code, not yet taken up, and I have great hope that some patriotic spirit will, at a favorable moment, call it up, and make it the key-stone of the arch of our government.

With respect to aristocracy, we should further consider, that before the establishment of the American States, nothing was known to history but the man of the old world, crowded within limits either small or overcharged, and steeped in the vices which that situation generates. A government adapted to such men would be one thing; but a very different one, that for the man of these States. Here every one may have land to labor for himself, if he chooses; or, preferring the exercise of any other industry, may exact for it such compensation as not only to afford a comfortable subsistence, but wherewith to provide for a cessation from labor in old age. Every one, by his property, or by his satisfactory situation, is interested in the support of law and order. And such men may safely and advantageously reserve to themselves a wholesome control over their public affairs, and a degree of freedom, which, in the hands of the *canaille* of the cities of Europe, would be instantly perverted to the demolition and destruction of everything public and private. The history of the last twenty-five years of France, and of the last forty years in America, nay of its last two hundred years, proves the truth of both parts of this observation.

But even in Europe a change has sensibly taken place in the mind of man. Science had liberated the ideas of those who read and reflect, and the American example had kindled feelings of right in the people. An insurrection has consequently begun, of science, talents, and courage, against rank and birth, which have fallen into contempt. It has failed in its first effort, because the mobs of the cities, the instrument used for its accomplishment, debased by ignorance, poverty and vice, could not be restrained to rational action. But the world will recover from the panic of this first catastrophe. Science is progressive, and talents and enterprise on the alert. Resort may be had to the people of the country, a more governable power from their principles and subordination; and rank, and birth, and tinsel-aristocracy will finally shrink into insignificance, even there. This, however, we have no right to meddle with. It suffices for us, if the moral and physical condition of our own citizens qualifies them to select the able and good for the direction of their government, with a recurrence of elections at such short periods as will enable them to displace an unfaithful servant, before the mischief he meditates may be irremediable.

I have thus stated my opinion on a point on which we differ, not with a view to controversy, for we are both too old to change opinions which are the result of a long life of inquiry and reflection; but on the suggestions of a former letter of yours, that we ought not to die before we have explained ourselves to each other. We acted in perfect harmony, through a long and perilous contest for our liberty and independence. A constitution has been acquired, which, though neither of us thinks perfect, yet both consider as competent to render our fellow citizens the happiest and the securest on whom the sun has ever shone. If we do not think exactly alike as to its imperfections, it matters little to our country, which, after devoting to it long lives of disinterested labor, we have delivered over to our successors in life, who will be able to take care of it and of themselves.

Of the pamphlet on aristocracy which has been sent to you, or who may be its author, I have heard nothing but through your letter. If the person you suspect, it may be known from the quaint, mystical, and hyperbolical ideas, involved in affected, new-fangled and pedantic terms which stamp his writings. Whatever it be, I hope your quiet is not to be affected at this day by the rudeness or intemperance of scribblers; but that you may continue in tranquillity to live and to rejoice in the prosperity of our country, until it shall be your own wish to take your seat among the aristoi who have gone before you. Ever and affectionately yours.